VIRGIL'S
BARBECUE
ROAD TRIP
COOKBOOK

VIRGIL'S

BARBECUE

ROAD TRIP COOKBOOK

The Best Barbecue from Around the Country
Without Ever Leaving Your Backyard

Neal Corman
with Chris Peterson

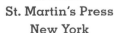

St. Martin's Press
New York

www.stmartins.com

Designed by Phil Mazzone
Food photographs by Alex Martinez
Photograph of Jeffrey Bank by Barry Morgenstein
Production Manager: Adriana Coada

Library of Congress Cataloging-in-Publication Data

Corman, Neal.
    Virgil's barbecue road trip cookbook : the best barbecue from around the country
without ever leaving your backyard / by Neal Corman with Chris Peterson. –1st ed.
        p. cm.
ISBN 978-1-250-04109-8 (hardcover)
ISBN 978-1-4668-3724-9 (e-book)
    1. Barbecuing—United States.
    I. Peterson, Chris, 1961- II. Virgil's Real Barbecue (Firm) III. Title. IV. Title.
    TX840.B3C668 2014
    641.7'6--dc23
                            2014000126
    e-ISBN 9781466837249

First Edition: April 2014

10   9   8   7   6   5   4   3   2   1

In loving memory of Artie Cutler, whose love of food and adventure taught me how to enjoy the journey.

—Alice Cutler

CONTENTS

3. DRINKS 81

4. SIDES 109

5. RUBS, MARINADES, AND SAUCES   155

6. BEEF   171

10. SWEETS 277

11. SUGGESTED MENUS 315

FOREWORD

Jeffrey Bank, CEO Alicart Restaurant Group

Living and working in New York City can be exciting, but it can also be stressful. There are days when you start out moving 100 miles per hour and things only get more hectic from there. That's especially true of the Alicart Restaurant Group, where we're opening some of the largest restaurants in the country.

My office is just down the street from our Virgil's Time Square location, and when the pressure cooker gets to be a bit much, I head over to Virgil's. The minute I walk through the doors, I start to unwind. It's like I've been transported to a simple barbecue joint in some small town and the rest of the world is on the outside looking in. I can loosen my tie, dive into the world's best comfort food, and just relax. I'm not alone. If you look around the Virgil's dining room during the height of the dinner rush, the first thing that strikes you is that everyone is happy. You'll see kids, senior citizens, as many women as men, whole families on their first trip to New York, and weary business travelers who have been to the city a million times before and are looking for a little taste of home. The two things that unite them all are barbecue and smiles.

They're smiling because at Virgil's, we've always focused on unique and authentic barbecue served in pleasant surroundings by people who care about the experience. From the first road trips our founder Artie Cutler took, to the constant research and experimentation our pitmasters continue to do, it's all about keeping it real. We think people know the difference. We have more than one Virgil's location, but we don't consider ourselves a chain. We think of ourselves as a few barbecue roadhouses not much different from any you might find on the back roads of North Carolina or in a small town outside of Austin. It's a much different way of looking at things, and of doing business, than any chain.

That comes through not just in the cooking but in the entire atmosphere of Virgil's. Our waitstaff and bartenders are likely to greet you as if you were a friend they haven't seen in a while. (That can be quite a surprise for people who expected something a little more curt from New York City.) They all know quite a bit about the food and they have ready answers to just about anything you could ask. They put as much into making people feel at home as the kitchen staff does into the food. And they take care with what comes out of the kitchen, because they understand how central great food is to the Virgil's experience. I can safely say our barbecue is second to none. But how and where we serve it turns a great meal into a fantastic experience.

I may not be the chef, but I certainly have what it takes to create true quality barbecue. As a businessman on the business end of the restaurant, I'd like nothing better than to be able to order boxes of frozen hush puppies, premade biscuit mix, and precut frozen fries. I could save a lot of money, time, and hassle. But all that isn't the Virgil's way. Our staff proudly uses the freshest ingredients they can find, and they make everything on our menu by hand. We smoke all our own barbecue on the premises.

That's the Virgil's I know and the one that is a sanctuary for me—and a lot of other people as well.

The staff at Virgil's long ago got in the habit of calling customers "visitors." Like, "How many visitors do we expect tonight?" It reflects our philosophy that the people who come into our restaurants every day are treated as well as you would treat friends and family at a Sunday afternoon cookout. People pick up on that. Like me, everyone who comes through Virgil's front doors visibly relaxes, moving a little slower and calmer and wearing a great big grin. That's what makes Virgil's more than a restaurant. We are part of an idea, the barbecue-culture notion that living should be easy and should focus on the things that truly matter—things like enjoying the company of family and friends, eating a hearty, good meal, and taking time to relax and recharge your batteries.

When we first started down the road that led to this book in your hands, I knew for certain that it had to embody more than just a selection of terrific barbecue recipes. It had to capture the spirit of barbecue and the spirit of Virgil's. The book had to be a door to a place where the clock ticks slower, quality is king, and the things that really matter are front and center. Not everyone has a Virgil's a block away for when they're feeling the need to truly unwind, take a breath, and enjoy terrific barbecue. So I wanted this book to help readers create a Virgil's of your very own in your backyard.

That's a lot to ask from a cookbook. But read through this one, and I think you'll agree that we've done it. We've picked the most popular dishes from our menu and put directions in simple, easy-to-follow language. We've also added a lot of interesting background about barbecue, and some tips and shortcuts to help you whip up perfect meals with less time and effort. Now, if you'll excuse me, I've got an ice-cold beer and some ribs waiting for me, and some unwinding to do.

—Jeffrey Bank

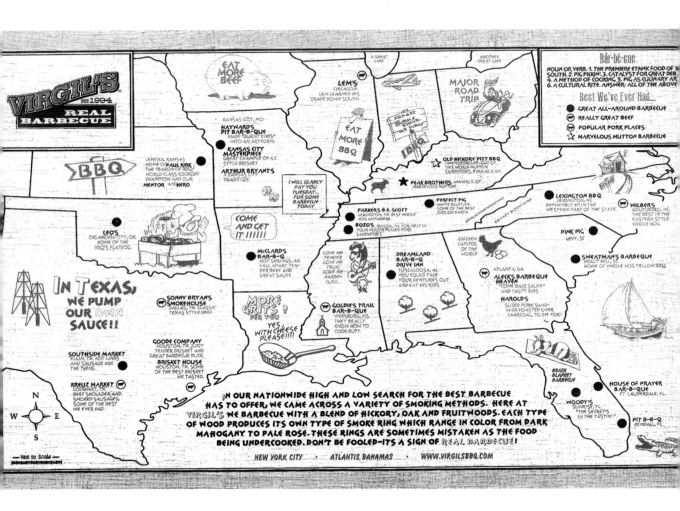

INTRODUCTION

The Hunt for Mouthwatering Barbecue

Virgil's Real Barbecue Restaurant stands at the "Crossroads of the World," better known as New York City's Times Square. That makes a lot of sense, given that Virgil's was founded by restaurateur Artie Cutler as a kind of "crossroads of barbecue." Back in 1994, there wasn't any authentic barbecue to be had in the Big Apple, and Artie wanted to bring the real deal right to the heart of the city he loved so much. It was a grand vision and a big challenge.

He knew that getting it right would mean some digging. You see, authentic barbecue is like a big old tree that grows from four different regional roots: Memphis, the Carolinas, Kansas City, and Texas. Artie understood that, and he wanted his restaurant's menu to feature signature dishes from all of those places. But developing the perfect menu and cooking everything just the way a local pitmaster would meant heading right to the source, actually visiting each region and checking out every different kind of barbecue, up close and personal.

So Artie set out on a road trip with his chef, general manager, and business partners. The gang flew to Memphis, rented a minivan, and started driving. Their motto became "follow the smoke," because if you saw a pillar of smoke from the road, there was sure as shootin' bound to be some memorable barbecue right underneath.

They'd pull into a dirt parking lot off a two-lane back road, pile out of the minivan, and crowd around some scarred-up picnic table to start tasting whatever was on the menu. They quickly learned to tell good from bad barbecue with just one bite.

That road trip took Artie's group across the South, from hole-in-the-wall places that were more smoke than lumber, to larger, legendary barbecue establishments. They ate tons of barbecue, good and bad. They sampled melt-in-your-mouth pulled pork, spareribs dripping with flavor, barbecued beer-can chicken, traditional smoked Texas brisket, and just about everything else that's ever found its way onto a grill. Over time, they began to really understand exactly what makes good barbecue and what makes great barbecue. They listened, and took notes, and asked for recipes and cooking tips—and, lo and behold, they got them (barbecue folk are nothing if not generous). More road trips followed. The road trips themselves set the stage for the success of Virgil's Real Barbecue Restaurant—founded in 1994 and still going strong.

The interior of the Times Square Virgil's before the chaos—and the fun—begins!

From the very start, Virgil's has been about happy people crowding around a table and making memories over great food. It's about enjoying the company of friends and family in a warm, welcoming atmosphere with the perfect eats on the table in front of every chair. But as happy and satisfied as our customers are, we know that there are a whole lot of people who just can't make it to the original Virgil's in New York City or any of our other Virgil's locations. So we figured we'd gather our best, most popular recipes, put 'em all down in a cookbook, and bring the restaurant to all those people who can't visit us in person!

We've driven hundreds upon hundreds of miles to find the very best dishes from all four points on the barbecue compass. We've filled up notebook after notebook, collected countless recipes and tips, tasted all the cooking we could find, and talked to pitmasters from East Kansas to West Texas. We've worked to get it just right because we aren't about to feed mediocre barbecue to the people we care about. We've put the sum of that hard-earned knowledge in this book, so you can cook nothing but the best for the people you care about.

Racks of ribs waiting for their turn in the smoker, and then onto some lucky customer's plate.

Hot-Smoked History

The truth is, ask three barbecue professionals what makes the best "true" barbecue, and you're likely to wind up with three distinctly different answers. At Virgil's we think it's easier than that. The "right" barbecue depends on personal preferences and which regional style seems tastiest to you. Period. Of course, it doesn't hurt to know a little bit about those different styles.

When you're talking authentic barbecue, you're talking about four regions: Memphis, the Carolinas, Kansas City, and Texas. All are fairly represented in the pages that follow. Each region has its own particular character and way of doing things. That's a consequence of history. Like America itself, the geography of barbecue has been influenced by immigrants. Early settlers from England, Czech butchers, Old West cow punchers, and Mexican farmhands have all put their stamp on the barbe-

cue of different states. Settlers who found it easier to let their pigs roam, slaughtering and cooking them out in the open, are why pork plays such a big part in Memphis and the Carolinas' barbecue. The presence of cattle in Texas as far back as anyone can remember is why beef is so important in that region's 'cue.

Memphis barbecue is all about the hog and, more often than not, all about ribs. (Matter of practicality—ribs are just easier to handle than a whole hog.) Traditionalists will tell you that Memphis ribs should be served dry and accompanied by the sound of a blues band. Ribs in this part of the country are treated only with a dry rub before cooking, and they are generally eaten without sauce. This lets the meat's incredibly rich natural flavor shine through. The spices and smoke used in barbecuing Memphis ribs are meant only to accent the natural sweetness of the pork. If a sauce is served with the ribs, chances are it'll be pretty understated, with ketchup used as a base. They may serve them dry in Memphis, but we don't mind when our customers slather sauce over our ribs. Eat 'em how you like 'em.

The Carolinas, on the other hand, tend to go whole hog. The most common Carolina barbecue is super-tender pork pulled and chopped to a fine consistency. Unlike in Memphis, sauce in the Carolinas is considered religion, and regional variations abound. Basically, though, you'll find three types: vinegar-based sauces with strong peppery seasonings and chili powder that will make the sauce red and hot; sauces based on tomato or ketchup, creating a sweeter, tamer flavor; and mustard-based sauces with a hot body and complex flavors.

Barbecued chicken is just about as good as a bird can get.

Texas is all about the steer. Beef cuts dominate and, where once upon a time a whole cow would be slow cooked over a pit, modern Texas barbecue centers on the easier-to-handle and easier-to-cook brisket. Authentic Texas barbecue is usually served dry, so that dry rub spices (and sometimes, the "mop" used to baste the meat during cooking) add flavor to the meat while it's barbecuing and help keep it moist. Texas is the biggest state in the union, which means that you'll see a lot of variation on that theme. You can still find roadside meat markets that serve up barbecued sausage just like the good ol' boys used to do—all alone on white butcher paper with crackers or white bread as a side. Any time a Texas barbecue joint serves up a sauce, it's likely to be tomato-based and smoky (keep in mind that Texas borders the land of the ancho chili and chipotle). You'll also find devoted grill jockeys in the Longhorn State, men who like nothing better than a nice juicy steak cooked rare over direct heat. And who doesn't?

We smoke our 'cue like they do throughout the Southern barbecue belt—with real hickory and fruit woods that give meat, pork, and chicken incredible flavors.

Kansas City is the region and style most affected by the other regions—and blending elements of those areas—because it was the last place of the four to find its barbecue voice. Kansas City pitmasters tend to do their barbecue wet, and sauces are a big part of KC's recipes. They like their sauce tomato-based, a bit sweet, and not overly spicy. Kansas City is also known for its chicken, fried and otherwise.

 Oval Office Barbecue

You may think of barbecuing as a pretty "regular guy" pursuit all in all, but U.S. presidents from Thomas Jefferson to George W. Bush have all been big fans. In fact, Texas's own Lyndon Baines Johnson made history in 1964, when he asked legendary cowboy-style barbecue master Walter Jetton to cook a big splashy State Dinner honoring Mexico's President-elect Gustavo Díaz Ordaz. The meal was held outside on LBJ's ranch tucked alongside the Pedernales River. Jetton barbecued brisket, ribs, chicken, and sausage for 250 guests the old-fashioned way— slowly, over open pits above or in the ground, full of hot coals. As important as all those folks might have been, barbecue is the great equalizer. They ate theirs the same way most Texas cowboys originally did—standing up, using just the utensils they were born with.

All these regions mean there's a lot to choose from when deciding what you're going to barbecue and how you're going to cook it. You may prefer to barbecue the traditional way, "low and slow" over indirect heat. Or you might be one of the legions of backyard grillers who prefer to cook small cuts of meat quickly over direct heat. In either case, you can choose to cook with or without smoke (and we're going to tell you how).

We're not ones to judge, so we've accommodated all the different tastes and interpretations of barbecue within the chapters of this book. Once you get to turning the pages that follow, you're going to find traditional barbecue recipes from the four major regions, as well as simpler grilling recipes. You'll find a lot more as well—we've thrown in a boatload of recipes for side dishes, drinks, desserts, and the like. (Purists aside, most people simply don't live by the main course alone!) We've been careful to include something for every taste, appetite, and cooking preference. The idea is to make memorable cookout meals, not just memorable barbecue. That's the way we do it at Virgil's, and it seems to work. It's usually hard to hear yourself think over the laughter and conversation in our dining rooms.

In the end, the best yardstick by which to judge your barbecue are the big wide smiles of the people eating it. If what you serve makes an unforgettable get-together out of any given day, with lots of happy stomachs as the sun goes down . . . well then, heck, that was the right barbecue for you.

Start with the Flame

It's no accident that we put all the gear information, along with the basics of barbecuing, right up in the front of this book. Any great cookout starts with the type of cooking you're comfortable doing, and the type of equipment you want to do it on. Don't you worry, though, you won't hear anyone at Virgil's suggesting you run out and get an old oil drum to cut up and make a true country cooker. We will, however, explain in simple terms how to do just about any type of barbecue—from the densest smoking to quick-and-easy grilling—on the unit that sits out back of your place right now. The basics of barbecuing are fairly fundamental. There's two ways to do it: with direct heat right over the fuel source, or with indirect heat with the fuel source off to the side of what you're cooking. Simple as that. Well, mostly.

Chapter 1 will explain it all in much more detail, but honestly, if barbecuing were a big to-do and a whole lot of hassle, do you really think so many people would be so darned crazy for it?

★ What's in a Name? ★

Fans of barbecue love to have friendly disagreements about the best style, the best cut, and the best wood for smoking, but there's just as much disagreement about where the name of this particularly American cooking style comes from. Mexican *vaqueros* (cowboys) took to wrapping sheep or cow heads in maguey leaves, and burying them in big pits full of smoldering coals to slow cook for hours. They called the tender, smoky meat *barbacoa*, a word that can be traced even further back to the Caribbean Taino culture—there the word for "sacred fire pit" was *barabicu*. Fans of France are much more likely to go with the theory that the French word *barbe à queue* ("beard to tail," meaning the whole hog) led to the English "barbecue." Maybe you even have your own theory. But as far as everyone at Virgil's is concerned, you can call it hokeypokey if you want, just as long as it has the unique, smoky, tongue-pleasing flavors that you can only get by cooking with smoke and flame!

Pick Your 'Cue

Once you've settled on your chosen way of cooking, it's time to pick the delicious dishes you'll be serving up. Everyone should follow his or her own hunger when barbecuing, but here's how we'd suggest you use this book.

Start by choosing your main course. Got a hankering for beef? Turn to chapter 6 and pick out our traditional Texas brisket if you feel like taking the slow route. You won't find a deeper, smokier flavor and more distinctive surface texture (pros call it the "bark"). Want to speed things up a bit? Grill up a few Virgil's burgers for an easy meal that can land on the bun in a matter of minutes. In any case, let your main course take center stage and lead the rest of your decisions. Select starters, sides, and desserts that compliment the flavors of your 'cue and can be made in the time you've set aside. We've included some full menus in the last chapter, to help you create meals that are greater than the sum of their parts.

Let's not forget, though, that a big part of the fun is bringing your own creativity

to the whole shebang. Don't you hesitate to experiment with your own rubs, sauces, and marinades, or try out different woods for smoking. We strongly suggest you read chapters 1 and 5 first, though. They should give you a good idea of how to build appealing flavor blends and how to ensure the tenderest barbecue possible.

Thirst being as strong as hunger, we think a little liquid refreshment is a pretty essential part of any cookout. That's why we've included a whole chapter full of fun drinks that are perfectly suited to the flavors in barbecue. To make the liquid part of the meal even easier, we've added beer-pairing suggestions after every main-course recipe.

As you make your way through these various chapters, you'll find a passel of tips and hints to make your barbecuing easier, quicker, and more enjoyable. We've also added some interesting and entertaining background about some of barbecue's most famous moments, its best tall tales, and a few of the more unusual characters to light up a smoker or fire pit.

The whole idea is to help you cook the barbecue that appeals most to you, your family, and your friends. You don't necessarily have to do it exactly the way we do, as long as you get the basics right. Add your own spice here and there, mix up a slaw with your own variations, or whatever. The point isn't to fret about messing up your barbecue. As long as you, your family, and your friends all enjoy it, you got it right!

 'Cue Fun Fact

The most popular days for barbecuing are the Fourth of July, Memorial Day, and Labor Day, in that order. Sort of makes sense when you think about it, because those holidays essentially represent the middle, and either end of the sweet, sweet summer season.

1

The Art (and a Little Bit of Science) of Barbecue

At Virgil's, we do most of our barbecuing in two fourteen-hundred-pound Southern Pride smokers. When we fill them up, you can smell the woodsmoke and barbecued meat all over Times Square. These bad boys are ideal for maintaining the perfect temperature and conditions we need to produce our consistently world-class barbecue. If you're going to turn out hundreds of barbecued meals a night like we do, you absolutely need some heavy-duty equipment in the kitchen. We feed hickory and apple wood into the firebox and smoke fills a cooking chamber as big as a Buick. It's quite a sight to see. (If you're ever in New York's Times Square, stop on by and we'll be glad to show you!)

The firebox in one of our smokers eats a lot a wood, but makes for some sweet smoke flavoring in our barbecue.

But all of us at Virgil's also have our own rigs at home, and we understand that most folks will be working with the grill that's already sitting in the backyard. Even if you're ready for an upgrade, chances are you'll want to cook with the fuel that you're used to, on a unit that is meant for home use. We may own the cookers to top all cookers, but that doesn't mean we don't understand how to cook up great barbecue on more modest gear. Truth is, in our many road trip travels, we've seen some awfully delicious barbecue come out of some amazing—and amazingly simple—pieces of equipment. That's just one of the many great things about barbecuing: the techniques remain the same, no matter what type of cooker you're using.

There's plenty of room in the cookout for grilled and barbecued fare; a quick-seared burger is one of the best foods of summer.

Our founder Artie Cutler used to tell one story in particular, about great cooking on humble equipment. He and a group of other Virgil's adventurers were driving the back roads of Tennessee, on the hunt for great barbecue, when they pulled into a gas station on some woodsy stretch of two-lane highway. While the rental cars were getting gassed up, he stretched his legs and caught sight of a little homemade barbecue stand off to the side of the station. It looked pretty much like a snow cone stand you might see on a seashore boardwalk, except that this particular establishment was manned by a single oversized fella wearing bib overalls and nothing else. This gentleman had built a pit from cinder blocks, grates, and corrugated tin sheets right there in the service station parking lot. Our fearless leader, being the brave wanderer that every Virgil's road tripper must be, ordered up the only thing on the menu—a pulled pork sandwich. That roadside chef removed the corrugated tin to reveal a whole pig lying there, just smoking over a bed of coals. He pulled some meat off that pig with his bare hands, slapped it on a bun, and put it on a plate with a little sauce. Wouldn't you know it? It turned out to be the best pulled pork the Virgil's crew tasted that whole darn trip. Cinder blocks and corrugated tin. Go figure.

So, no, you certainly don't need some fancy, superdeluxe rig with all the latest gizmos to whip up some fine barbecue. The unit you have in your backyard can probably be used to cook everything you would want to put on a fire. Of course, if that unit isn't the right size or is just a little too long in the tooth, then it might be time to look around for a cooker that better suits your cookout purposes.

The rugged bark on a perfectly smoked brisket is what keeps the meat tender and juicy.

Either way, you'll find the lowdown on the different types of barbecues you can choose from, along with a summary of the pros and cons of each type, in the next few pages. We wrap up this chapter with the basics of grilling and barbecuing, offering you some inside advice on how to get exactly the results you're after, whether you're searing up a nice rare steak or cooking a mouthwatering brisket low and slow.

The Gear

When it comes to the equipment you use for backyard cookouts, size does matter. You have to consider the amount of cooking you're going to do before you can decide if your current cooker is up to the job. You may need a replacement if you intend to tackle large cuts of meat like a brisket or oversized, whole fish, or if you have lots of friends and will regularly need to cook a gigantic tableful of food for your get-togethers.

Regardless of size, you'll be a happier cook if you're working on a properly constructed grill. Certain indicators of quality are common to all grills. The best have adjustable grates that are removable for easy cleaning. The grates themselves can be stainless steel, bare cast iron, or porcelain-coated cast iron. We much prefer stainless steel grates because they are the easiest to clean, even though cast-iron grates have excellent heat-retention properties and work well for searing grilled foods (even if they are a bit heavy and cumbersome to handle and move around). Cast-iron grates also need to be reseasoned regularly. Porcelain-coated cast-iron grates are easy to clean up and hold heat well, but the porcelain eventually chips—which is why we usually stay away from them. If your grates are two exits down the road from beat-up and grimy, get yourself new grates. They aren't going to set you back much, and the quality of your barbecue is at stake!

★ Seasoning Cast Iron Grates ★

Cast iron is just about the perfect material for barbecue grill grates because it retains heat like nobody's business. But if you want to keep cooking and cleanup as simple and straightforward as possible, you'll need to regularly "season" the grates. Seasoning is the process of sealing the microscopic pores of the iron, and when done right it makes for a nearly nonstick surface. Before seasoning your grates, make sure they're absolutely clean, dry, and free of rust. Next, saturate a paper towel with pure safflower, corn, or canola oil and rub the grates with the towel, coating them completely. If you're using a gas grill, preheat the grill with the burners set to medium, then set the grates in place and leave the burners on for about an hour. Turn the burners off and let the grates cool down naturally. For charcoal grill grates, light the coals and put the grate in place. Leave the vents open and let the coals burn for an hour. Then close the vents to extinguish the coals. Keep in mind that over time the surface of cast iron degrades. That means you'll need to thoroughly clean the grates and reseason them every summer—and sometimes two to three times a year if you are a heavy griller and you notice your barbecue is starting to stick to the grill. You can help keep you grates clean in between seasonings by oiling the food (not the grate) whenever you're cooking on the grill. Before you start barbecuing, crank up the grill, burn everything off the grates, and brush 'em clean. Also keep in mind that the key to not having protein stick to grates is to not move the food around until the surface of the food has seared and caramelized to the point that it's easy to move!

You'll also want to look for signs of solid construction. Keep an eye out for full welds, rather than spot welds, and smooth, even seams. If you regularly move your grill around, you'll want to make sure the wheels are solid rubber with thick solid metal axles. A lined hood is a big bonus, and handles should be wrapped with wood or a protective sleeve of some sort to prevent burns. The best grills, regardless of the type of fuel used, include a thermometer so you can quickly determine the temperature inside the cooking chamber (and you want a thermometer that reads actual numbers rather than zones). Looking past these basics, you'll be choosing a (or using your existing) grill from one of the following.

 Grill Real Estate

When you're shopping for a new grill or trying to determine if your current one is going to meet your cookout needs, there are some simple guidelines grill manufacturers have put together to make things a little easier.

Number of Folks to Feed	Suggested Grill Size
Up to 4	300 to 450 in^2
5 to 8	450 to 650 in^2
More than 8 (or large cuts)	650 or more in^2

Gas Grills. Propane-powered grills are the most popular type of outdoor grills sold in America. That's because they're just about as easy as it gets. There's no fussing with the fuel source, you have total control over the heat and flame, and you can start grilling with just a short warm-up period. You'll find lots and lots of fancy gas grills with all kinds of extras, but always start your search with the basics: the burners. For real barbecuing—low-and-slow cooking, that is—you absolutely have to have a gas grill with three or more burners so that you can position the food off to the side or between lit burners. The best burners are stainless steel or brass—cast iron are common on lower-priced gas grills but aren't as efficient as brass. Whether you need extra burners depends on the amount of barbecuing you tend to do, and how many people you're looking to cook for.

Use	Burners
The average griller/basic grill/small gatherings	3
Regular griller/big grill/large family	4
Super griller/super grill/big crowds	5 or more

All gas grill burners are covered by material that protects the burners themselves from juices and food remnants. This is either a metal heat diffuser or faux briquettes crafted of clay or lava rock. If possible, go with the heat diffuser; the juices vaporize when they hit the metal, flavoring the food and giving you a bit more of that authentic barbecue flavor. (Find more on how to get a true smoky flavor, on page 33.) Lava rocks will tend to break down and are darn near impossible to get clean.

Depending on how wide you're willing to open your wallet, you can choose from a whole lot of extras, but just be sure any add-ons make sense for the way you cook out.

Almost all gas grills these days include built-in thermometers (analog at low to mid range, digital at the high end). The best of these include a removable, instant-read thermometer so that you can test whatever you're barbecuing in addition to knowing how hot the cooking chamber is getting. Side shelves and warming plates can come in handy if you want to keep side dishes warm.

If you're a Virgil's type of avid griller—a cook that likes to use the grill more than the stove—you may want to upgrade to true side burners that allow you to do a full range of cooking right there at the grill. These let you heat up side dishes and keep them warm, or create specialty dishes like caramelized onions right alongside whatever it is you're barbecuing. Motorized, self-turning rotisseries are luxury features that can expand the way you barbecue. They are great ways to slow-cook large fish, or even the Thanksgiving turkey.

When it comes to gas grills, BTU ratings are often touted as a measure of how powerful and effective the grill will be. Sorry to say, it's not quite that clear cut. The BTUs of any given grill are actually a measure of how much fuel the grill uses. How effectively the grill heats up and stays hot is a reflection of how big the grates are and the number of burners in relation to the BTUs. BTUs will give you some idea of the relative power of the grill, but don't put too much weight on that particular number; beyond a certain point, the BTUs may not be relevant because cooking low and slow doesn't require a lot of extra power—just well-crafted, reliable burners and a well-sealed lid.

Any discussion about gas grill heat isn't complete without mentioning the relatively new technology of infrared burners. These heat up way quicker and get much hotter than traditional gas grill burners. If you want to see the Virgil's crew get in a real debate, just mention infrared burners. That's because traditionalists think they're unnecessary. If you plan on doing more grilling than barbecuing or smoking, infrared burners may serve you well and save some time in the process (they're great at searing small cuts of meat). But the fact is, infrared burners take some getting used to and some practice to master.

Keep in mind that propane isn't your only choice when it comes to gas grills. Natural gas grills are a less common option, but they allow you to plumb the grill right into the home's natural gas line—meaning you'll never have to refill a gas tank. The downside is that the grill can't be moved around once it's connected to the gas line and, of course, it's not an option if your house isn't serviced by natural gas.

Charcoal Grills. A charcoal grill is the unit of choice for traditionalist backyard barbecuers. Charcoal grilling is considered the best way to get that authentic smoky barbecue flavor, even if these types of grills take more work than a gas grill would. There's also a bit more cleanup with a charcoal grill because of the ash, and the fuel

★ Play It Safe ★

Never line the bottom tray or chute of a gas grill with foil—that's just asking for a grease fire. You need to keep the trap and grease pan clean for the same reason. If you've fallen a little behind on your cleaning chores and you experience a flare-up, stay calm. Move any food on the grates out of the way, turn the burners off, and let the fire burn out on its own. Fire safety is also an issue with how you handle your propane tanks. Never store them indoors, even in a garage, shed, or similar outbuilding.

itself can be slightly more expensive than gas. But, oh, that unique taste! If that's what you're after and you want to do it like the pros do, consider the following features when you go shopping for your charcoal grill.

Look for easy access to the firebox or charcoal compartment. Your life will be a whole lot simpler and you'll be a happier camper if you can add charcoal without having to move the food and grates around. You should also look for an easy-to-empty ash collector. A slide-out removable ash drawer is preferable, although vents that allow the ash to fall into an ash pan are almost as good. Scooping ashes out of the bottom of a low-cost unit will leave you wishing you had plunked down a little more coin. For maximum cooking control, you're going to want simple-to-operate top and bottom vents that can be opened or closed by degrees.

The type of charcoal you use is going to have an effect on how your barbecue tastes. Not all charcoal is created equal. Back in the day, barbecuers would cook their food over large open pits fueled by burning hardwoods. They'd wait a good long time for the wood to burn down and then cook over the charred embers that were left smoldering. You can still do it this way by buying authentic "charwood" charcoal made from different hardwoods (it's also called "lump charcoal"). You can find lump charcoal in different hardwoods for different flavors of smoke.

 From Car to 'Cue

You might be surprised to know that the standardized charcoal briquettes that are such a hallmark in backyard grills across the country weren't the invention of any barbecue old-timer or pitmaster. In fact, the simple fuel development that would go on to make grilling so convenient for home cooks everywhere is all thanks to automobile pioneer Henry Ford. In the 1920s, Mr. Ford was looking for ways to repurpose waste products produced in his manufacturing facilities. By using a refinement process developed earlier, he was able to cheaply and quickly transform the hardwood scraps left over from making Model T wheels and other auto parts into small, uniform pieces of charcoal. Originally known as "Ford's charcoal" and sold to commercial customers for coal-fired restaurant ovens and boilers, the product eventually found a market among home consumers. The "briquets" as they were called would eventually be marketed through Ford dealerships nationwide, and would generate millions in sales. E. G. Kingsford managed the Ford charcoal operation, and the company town where it was based was named after him. Which goes a far piece in explaining why, when the business was sold to some investors, they called their new corporation Kingsford Chemical Company. And why that name—instead of Ford's—still graces every bag of Kingsford charcoal briquettes.

A lot of people, on the other hand, prefer the ease and lower cost of charcoal "briquettes." These are uniform squares of pressed sawdust and other fillers. They're easy to work with and they can last twice as long as lump charcoal, but purists insist that you can't get the same smoky wood flavor from briquettes (although the technique on page 32 might take care of that objection).

No discussion about charcoal grills would be complete without mentioning the Kamado grill. This is a popular—and expensive—variation on the basic "clamshell" charcoal grill. The grill is shaped like an egg (the best known Kamado grill is actually called the Big Green Egg), with a ceramic shell encasing an inner liner. The design of the unit allows the grill to produce temperatures high enough for searing a grilled steak, while still being able to hold low temperatures steady for an extended period of time to smoke food. The Kamado grill has a lower firebox that can be refilled with charcoal through an access door, and top and bottom vents that draw smoke and heat up through the unit. Available in sizes from tiny to large enough to barbecue a twenty-pound turkey, Kamado grills are—owing to their complex design and construction—some of the priciest grills on the market.

Pellet Grills. This is the newest addition to the outdoor grill marketplace, and it's catching on. Pellet grills burn small, compressed wood pellets. The pellets are fed into a hopper, and then into a firebox at a preset rate. That rate determines the cooking heat, and gives you a lot of control over temperature—pellet grills are great for both direct-heat grilling and low-and-slow barbecuing. Because the pellets can be made from just about any wood, you can experiment with different flavors for your hot-smoked barbecue. The most widely available (and least expensive) pellets are a compressed combination of fruitwood and nonfruit hardwood such as oak. More expensive types are pure fruitwood, and you can use these sparingly to get whatever smoked flavor you're after.

The pellets themselves are easy to handle. Most pellet grills have a large hopper with an access door that makes refilling the pellets during cooking a breeze. Pellets

The Pro Choice

If you're competition-serious about your barbecuing, you might want to consider the unit many pros use—the offset cooker. This is essentially a smaller version of the Southern Pride smokers we use in our Virgil's restaurants. The firebox is separate from the cooking chamber, and the unit is fueled by pieces of hardwood fed directly into the firebox. The heat and smoke are drawn into the cooking chamber by a vent, hot smoking your barbecue in the process. Although you can buy offset cookers, many people (including many pros) make their own from steel drums or other large containers.

are also clean burning. However, the selection of pellets may be limited depending on where you live, and pellets are usually more expensive than charcoal or propane. Pellet grills are also generally more expensive than other types of grills, and if the pellet-feed mechanism breaks down, you're looking at a costly repair or replacement (a good reason to go with a higher-end pellet grill if you choose this option).

The Rest of Your Gear

A few simple but well-made tools can make barbecuing a whole lot easier. Put together your own barbecuing toolbox and keep your gear in working order to make sure your cookouts are as enjoyable, easy, and successful as possible.

- **Grill brush:** This utensil is essential no matter what grill you're using, but like all tools, it needs to be maintained. A lot of pros recommend buying a new one at the start of the season, but that depends on how often you grill, how sturdy the brush was to begin with, and what type of things you've cooked. One thing's for certain: you don't want bristles falling out of an overused brush and sticking to the grate—or finding their way into your food. We recommend replacing any brush that has loose bristles or other structural damage. In any case, you'll be using this every time you fire up the grill, so spend a little more for a quality grill brush with a nice wide head and a long handle that's comfortable to hold.

- **Thermometer:** Make no mistake, you need a thermometer to properly barbecue. Actually, you need two (although depending on the thermometer, it might be able to do double duty). For any true low-and-slow cooking, you have to know and keep track of the temperature in your cooking chamber. Grill chamber temps that yo-yo up and down are sure to lead to bad barbecue. But you'll also need to measure the temperature of whatever it is your cooking—checking the internal temperature is really the only way you'll know if it's done (and if it's safe to eat). Buy yourself a good-quality instant read thermometer—either a probe type or a digital wireless. Then use it whenever you barbecue.

- **Utensils:** Tools dedicated to outdoor cooking will go an awful long way to making your life easier. Buy and use utensils specifically meant for barbecuing and you won't be caught short with tongs that can't turn the brisket, or a spatula that bends under the weight of a turkey breast. The basic set consists of a large rigid spatula, strong fork, and sturdy tongs that can hold a large cut of meat. The handles for all of these should be long enough to keep your hand away from the heat of the coals or fire, with nonslip, easy-to-clean grips.

- **Chimney starter:** An incredibly simple "must-have" if you're cooking with charcoal, the starter is a metal tube with a small lower chamber, a larger upper

★ Staying Safe ★

No matter what type of grill you use, they all kick off a mess of heat and can be dangerous if used incorrectly. Every year thousands of fires and millions of dollars in damages are caused by barbecue grills. Running the kind of large-scale cookers we do at Virgil's—in the crowded quarters of New York's Time Square neighborhood—we make safety our first concern. We want you to think safety first, too; don't you go being a statistic.

✓ **Get a fire extinguisher.** Always, always, always keep a fire extinguisher handy for that one-in-a-million event where things get away from you. Use a Class B or Class ABC rated fire extinguisher, and read the instructions *before* you need to use the extinguisher.

✓ **Choose the right location.** It's not just the grates that get hot; grills can produce serious temperatures on the back, bottom, and even sides of the unit. That's why you want to position your grill well away from any flammable material such as wood siding or decking (firefighting professionals recommend ten feet of clearance). Allow for plenty of air circulation around the grill, and make sure it's well out of the flow of foot traffic.

✓ **Keep it on the level.** No matter where you put your grill, make sure it's sitting level and stable. You don't want a simple clumsy moment ruining your cookout meal or starting a fire.

✓ **Know your grill.** A fire emergency isn't the time to be grabbing your grill's manual and figuring out how to properly deal with the problem. Read the manual before you ever start cooking.

✓ **Suit up right.** Avoid wearing long-sleeve shirts, loose clothing, or any garments that are highly flammable (just one more reason to leave that polyester disco shirt in the closet). And always use protective grilling mitts when working with your 'cue.

chamber, and a sturdy wooden handle. Fill the bottom with crumpled newspaper and the top with charcoal briquettes or lump charcoal, and light it up. You'll have hot coals in minutes, and it works sure as shooting every time. No need for that nasty lighter fluid that adds chemical flavors to your food! If you're barbecuing big meals, it may pay to get two of these for when you need to fire up a large batch of coals.

- **Timer:** Cooking times vary quite a bit, depending on what you're cooking, how consistent the heat is, and other factors. But having a timer near your grill is a good idea for cooking sensitive food like fish fillets or small pieces of chicken, and it can keep you aware of longer cooking times so you avoid that sin of sins: dried out, overcooked barbecue.

- **Barbecue lighter:** Trigger-activated barbecue lighters are simple as can be, but useful as all get-out. Just click the trigger to light a flame at the end of the long barrel, and you can light anything that needs igniting with a lot less fuss than matches would require. These work with gas grills that don't have an electric igniter, and with charcoal grills of all kinds.

- **Electric starter:** This is a paddle-shaped coil wand that you lay under your charcoal to get it going. You need an outlet nearby and you have to be sure to remove the starter once the coals get hot, or they'll melt the element. You might find this handy, but most barbecue enthusiasts are just as comfortable using a chimney starter or some other type of lighter.

Getting Down to the Cooking

Barbecue purists will tell you that true barbecue is cooked low and slow—a long time over moderate heat. But most backyard cooks enjoy grilling just as much. A simple seared steak can be a lot more practical for a quick weeknight cookout than a smoked pork butt.

At Virgil's we don't take sides. We see the beauty in all the different kinds of grill-based cooking. There's a place for quick-cooked grilled food, and a place for traditional barbecue standards like brisket. That's why we have such a big menu at Virgil's (which is how we've become such a New York institution), and why we've provided all manner of recipes in this book. And why we're about to explain how to cook fast or slow, hot or warm.

Grilling is essentially any cooking done on a grill over direct heat in excess of 350°F. True barbecue is cooked low and slow, usually entailing cooking indirectly (with the heat source off to the side of what's being cooked) for well more than an hour, at temperatures that are usually lower than 250°F. Grilling is better for quicker meals, more delicate foods such as shrimp and vegetables, and smaller cuts of meat. Barbecue tends to be a more leisurely affair that can take up the better part of a

We serve all tastes, including a little bit of barbecued pork, chicken, and brisket on our sampler plate. The right barbecue is the one you have a hankering for!

whole afternoon, and the best barbecue involves fairly large cuts of meat—from a beef brisket to a full rack of ribs to a complete chicken.

In either case, you need to preheat the cooking chamber: usually about twenty to thirty minutes for charcoal, ten to fifteen for gas. Gas burners are obviously easier to control, but once you get the hang of charcoal, it's pretty simple. Control the temperature in a charcoal grill by opening the vents (causing the coals to burn hotter and faster) or by closing them, and by the amount of charcoal you keep on the fire. You'll always know your coals are ready when they are covered in a fine gray ash.

Indirect Cooking. Regardless of whether you're a propane type of guy, a big fan of charcoal, or breaking in a brand-new pellet grill, the technique of cooking with indirect heat is going to be the same. The idea is to situate whatever it is that you're cooking away from the heat source. At Virgil's, we do that by having the fire in a separate firebox, with a ventilation system that draws the smoke into the cooking chamber. But you can use the same theory at home. In a charcoal grill, this usually means mounding the charcoal around the perimeter or off to one side of the grill, with no charcoal directly under the food. For a gas grill, it means turning off the burner directly under the food and leaving the others lit.

True barbecuing with indirect heat also means monitoring and controlling the temperature over the long period it takes to cook the food. This can be a bit of a chal-

Good Wood

The wood you choose for smoking your barbecue makes a big difference in how the final product tastes. Widely available nonfruit hardwoods like oak and hickory are popular because they're cheap and, well, widely available. But fruitwoods can put a distinctive taste on your barbecue and it pays to experiment to find the one that gives you a favorite flavor. You can use cherry, apple, pear, peach, and even more exotic citrus woods, all of which will lend their own special flavoring to your barbecue. The New York City Virgil's in Times Square burns a whole lot of wood, in a three-to-one mix of hickory with seasonal fruitwoods (usually apple or cherry). It gives our 'cue a unique, deep flavor with a hint of fruit.

lenge, depending on your fuel source and the grill you're using. Monitor the temperature regularly and add fuel as needed to keep things cooking along at the same pace. True barbecuing is done between 200°F and 300°F. Once the cooking temperature drops significantly lower than 200°F, you're into cold smoking territory (closer to curing than cooking the food), and over 300°F is where fast grilling is done. For more exact temperatures and the proper internal temperatures of whatever you are cooking, check the individual recipes in the pages that follow and the USDA guidelines on page 33.

Of course, there are other ways to cook food indirectly. Just remember that no matter how you arrange things on the grill, indirect cooking always requires the top of the grill to be closed, so that you create a chamber to trap the heat and smoke.

Now here's one of the most important points for the home cook who wants that true smoked flavor. In the case of gas or charcoal briquettes, this is usually done by soaking hardwood chips in water, then wrapping them in foil to create a packet, punching holes in the packet, and laying it on the heat source. The wood steams and burns slightly, releasing smoke that flavors the meat.

Another device used in indirect-heat barbecuing is a drip tray. Most of us at Virgil's tend not to use one for our own home barbecue, but you might want to try it out and see how it works for you. A drip tray is just a disposable aluminum pan you place under the meat to catch the fat drippings. It's a way to keep the grill clean and stop flare-ups from searing your smoked barbecue. Some cooks—including some pros—fill drip trays with beer, apple juice, or a blend of liquid ingredients that slowly evaporates, keeping the barbecue moist and helping to flavor it. Drip trays can also serve as heat deflectors if your grill is too small—or what you're cooking is too large—to keep the food away from the heat source. Finally, remember that if the indirect heat source is off to one side or another of the food, plan on both flipping and rotating the food to ensure even cooking.

Grilling. Grilling over direct heat is a much quicker affair than barbecuing, and involves a higher temperature, but the setup is actually similar. In the case of a charcoal grill, you create two to three levels of coals—from low to high. Start out by searing the food briefly, and then move it to an area of less heat to cook the meat the rest of the way without burning it (and perhaps to a third area to keep it warm while other cuts finish cooking). The same thing is done on a gas grill by setting different burners at different heats.

Grilling is the method of choice for relatively small cuts of meat and chicken, and for fish and vegetables. Learning to tell when a grilled food is done is part art and part science. You'll find more specific instructions in the recipes that follow.

The Special Case of True Smoking. Although you know you've hit the mark with your barbecue when it has a distinctively smoky flavor, the smoke used in the process is about just that—flavoring. Smoking, on the other hand, is the process of using the smoke to actually cure, or cook, the meat. Authentic smoking differs from both grilling and barbecuing. Although the smoke in barbecue can penetrate deep into the meat, truly smoked meat will be entirely saturated with the flavor of the particular wood you used. In addition, smoking is done with a smoker that confines the fuel source to a completely separate compartment. Smoking takes many hours and even days, and requires a lot of attention to maintain a steady, low temperature.

Once you've got your cooker sorted out and have your gear ready, the next step is the actual cooking. So what are you waiting for? Let's move into the next chapter and jump into some genuine cookout recipes. It's time to get your 'cue on.

Virgil's Grillin' Tips

Those people over at the USDA have kindly come up with guidelines for doneness, aimed at making sure anything you grill is safe to eat.

✓ **Pork:** Cook to 145°F (measured before removing from heat), *and allow for at least a three-minute rest*. These instructions are relatively new, and that "resting" part is not only good for flavor saturation, it gives the meat a chance to continue cooking for a short time. This recommendation includes all kinds of pork, from tenderloin to pork butt.

✓ **Meat** (including beef and lamb): Cook to 145°F, also with at least a three-minute rest.

✓ **Ground Meat** (of any type): Cook to 165°F, no rest necessary.

✓ **Poultry:** Cook to 165°F. Includes any kind of fowl, from chicken to wild turkey.

Obviously, how you measure that temperature is crucial to getting it right. Use an instant-read meat thermometer, and insert the probe into the thickest part of the cut, making sure to avoid bones and gristle that could skew the temperature. Hold the probe steady until you get a clear and constant temperature.

2

Starters and Salads

There are certainly more than a few experienced pitmasters who would say that a true barbecue meal should include only what comes off the grill. That's an old-time sentiment, from back in the day when a lot of barbecue joints were just converted meat markets serving up whatever they had cooked up that day and not much else besides crackers and pickles. With all due respect to history, at Virgil's we see barbecue as the center of the table; there's still plenty of room for a little something different to start out the meal.

You see, part of the reason people love to eat at Virgil's—whether they're in Times Square or in the Bahamas—is the sense of fun, the spirit of community and celebration we capture. Every night's just a great big enjoyable gathering of hungry people looking to have a simple, good time. We feel that the best way to have a celebration around food is to have lots of different options. That's the way we do things at Virgil's. Our starters and salads are just the first part of the whole show.

Barbecue starters should set the stage for the main course. The whole idea is to rev up your hunger. Our starters—and even our salads—give you a taste of the things to come off the grill or out of the smoker. No matter what they taste like, though, Virgil's starters are hearty fare. The one thing that unites all the different people coming through our front door is a healthy hunger. We aim to satisfy that with every course. That's why many of our starters can stand in as weeknight meals all by themselves, or be broken into a greater number of smaller servings.

Along with some classic starters, we've included our most popular salads. People generally think of coleslaw and potato salad when they think of barbecue, but we like to get a little more creative than that. Our salads are flavor explosions all by themselves, and can be meals on their own when there isn't time to throw something on the grill or you're just feeling like a one-dish dinner.

In any case, we focused this chapter on our easiest and tastiest recipes, dishes that aren't a big chore to make and still deliver plenty of bang for the buck. These recipes will also naturally complement the flavors of whatever barbecue you're serving. Whether you're using them to kick off a barbecue cookout, as handy standalone meals on any given weeknight, or even as part of a non-barbecue potluck (although we can't imagine such a thing!), there's just no wrong way to serve up these tasty dishes.

Maryland's Finest Crab Cakes

Variety is the spice of both life and barbecue, and that's why a little seafood appetizer is a great way to start off a meat-heavy cookout. These crispy crowd pleasers wrap the rich, sweet goodness of crab in a crisp, lightly breaded shell that will leave your gang calling for more. We make our crab cakes in the traditional Maryland "restaurant" style—pan fried with a minimum of filler and served undressed, no hamburger bun required (Maryland's "boardwalk" style makes a sandwich out of the starter). The spices we use are a Virgil's original composition, and they give the cake a little zing without overwhelming the naturally rich flavor of the crab. You can customize this starter to suit the occasion. Put your own spin on the spice blend or make smaller cakes to ensure guests don't get filled up before the main course or to use them as party treats. (Smaller is often better when working with expensive seafood like crab!) If you want the cakes to be as easy to handle as possible, do what we do—refrigerate them for about an hour before frying.

Serves 4–6

3 eggs

½ cup finely diced green bell pepper

½ cup thinly sliced green onion, greens only

1 cup seasoned bread crumbs (recommended: Progresso)

⅔ cup mayonnaise

1 tablespoon hot sauce

1 tablespoon Virgil's Creole Seasoning (page 160)

2 tablespoons Worcestershire sauce

2 pounds lump crab meat

2 tablespoons vegetable oil

1 cup Virgil's Remoulade (see box, page 40)

1. Whip the eggs in a large bowl until they double in volume. Add the remaining ingredients, except for the crab meat, oil, and remoulade. Mix well.

2. With a rubber spatula, gently fold in the crab meat. Be careful to avoid breaking it up.

3. Line a sheet pan with parchment paper. Use an ice cream scoop to form the crab cakes and place them on the sheet pan, leaving about ½ inch between the cakes. Cover with plastic and refrigerate until cool.

4. Preheat the oven to 400°F.

5. Heat the vegetable oil in a shallow pan over medium-high heat. Sauté the crab cakes in batches, flipping them when browned on the bottom. When the second side is browned, remove to the baking sheet.

6. When all the cakes have been browned, bake for 8 to 10 minutes. Remove and serve warm with Virgil's Remoulade on the side.

 **THE RIGHT BEER:** Rich delicious crab, even fried, calls for a crisp and refreshing brew. Something citrusy will work, such as a wheat beer that is not too spiced. We recommend lagers, pale ales, and wheats such as Magic Hat Circus Boy (*hefeweizen*), Rogue Dead Guy Ale (pale ale), Coney Island Lager, and Lone Star Beer (another lager).

A French Import

Remoulade is France's version of tartar sauce, and it's been a part of cookouts in the Creole South since right after the Revolutionary War. Barbecue folks being who they are, they just have to make it their own. That's how we feel at Virgil's, so we've created a signature remoulade that is a bit more like a hybrid between tartar sauce and barbecue sauce. The guests that fill our Times Square dining rooms just love putting this sauce on seafood of all sorts, and we're betting you will, too.

Virgil's Remoulade

2 egg yolks

1½ cups blended olive/canola oil (half and half)

2 tablespoons finely chopped celery

2 tablespoons finely chopped scallions, greens only

1 tablespoon finely chopped fresh parsley

1 tablespoon horseradish, drained well

Juice of ½ lemon

1 tablespoon Creole mustard

1½ teaspoons Worcestershire sauce

1½ teaspoons ketchup

1 teaspoon Dijon mustard

1 teaspoon white vinegar

1½ teaspoons hot sauce

1 teaspoon minced garlic

½ teaspoon sweet paprika

½ teaspoon kosher salt

Add the egg yolks to a medium mixing bowl, and slowly add the oil in a thin stream while continuously whisking. Fold in the remaining ingredients and refrigerate overnight. This will make 3 cups of remoulade, which may be more than you need. Use any extra with grilled shrimp, steamed or grilled fish, or even on cheeseburgers for a unique burger experience.

Popcorn Shrimp

These little fellas are tasty as all get-out and you'll find that even cookout guests who normally avoid seafood will dive right into these. The shrimp we use aren't the big prawns you'd see in a shrimp cocktail, but the smaller—and very tasty—rock shrimp variety. (If you can't find rock shrimp in your local seafood store or supermarket, you can substitute bay shrimp.) You're going to love how easy and quick these are to make, and how they are the ideal kickoff to just about any type of barbecue. We find that most popcorn shrimp recipes are kind of bland and rely on the breading to carry the day all by itself. Whereas most restaurants just bread the shrimp and leave it at that, we've added the popcorn to "popcorn shrimp," which is why kids and adults alike get a big kick out of this dish. We like to spice it up so you have a little flavor explosion in every bite. Fair warning, though, you may need to double the recipe to keep your crowd happy.

Serves 4

Popcorn

3 tablespoons vegetable oil

½ cup popcorn kernels

½ teaspoon crushed red pepper flakes

¼ teaspoon kosher salt

Shrimp

⅔ cup buttermilk

¼ cup hot sauce

3 teaspoons Virgil's Creole Seasoning (page 160), divided

1 cup Universal Flour (page 167)

¾ pound cleaned rock shrimp

½ cup or more vegetable oil

½ cup Virgil's Remoulade (page 40)

½ lemon

1. Heat the vegetable oil in a medium pot over medium heat. Add the popcorn kernels and heat for one minute.

2. Add the red pepper flakes and salt, and cover the pot. Shake occasionally while the popcorn pops, to keep it from burning. When the popping has stopped, remove to a large bowl.

3. Mix the buttermilk, hot sauce, and 2 teaspoons of the Creole Seasoning in a small bowl. Set aside.

4. Mix the Universal Flour and remaining Creole Seasoning in a small bowl. Set aside.

5. Dredge the shrimp in the buttermilk batter and drain off the excess, then dust in the flour mix until well coated. Knock off the excess.

6. Heat a deep fryer or a large saucepan filled with 1½ inches of vegetable oil (½ cup or more as necessary, depending on the size of the pan) to 350°F. Fry the shrimp (in batches to avoid crowding) for 2 minutes or until golden brown. Remove to a plate lined with paper towels.

7. Place the popcorn in a serving dish and top with the shrimp. Serve with Virgil's Remoulade on the side, and a squeeze of the lemon.

THE RIGHT BEER: A tart beer or refreshing lager works best to wash down these crunchy fried shrimp. We recommend pale ales and lagers such as the Full Sail Session Lager, Anchor Steam Beer, or Goose Island Sofie (Belgian-style ale).

Virgil's Kitchen Tip

Home cooks often have a heck of a time frying food if they don't have a dedicated fryer. Trouble is, most people don't get the oil hot enough. Heat up your oil and then test it by sprinkling in a small amount of bread crumbs. If the bread crumbs jump and sizzle, it's a good bet your oil is hot enough. If you're the type that likes things a little more precise, well shoot, go ahead and use a cooking thermometer—ideal frying temp is around 350°F. In any case, just be real, real careful around hot oil. Even if the oil isn't visibly sizzling, it can be hot enough to cause severe burns (we're talking from experience here). Stand back from the pan when you add food like the shrimp in our Popcorn Shrimp, and use tongs, not your hands. Slide the food into the pan rather than dropping it, and keep a close watch on it to avoid burning.

Virgil's Smoked Chicken Wings with Blue Cheese Dip

Our version of this traditional bar snack goes heavy on the rich, smoky flavor and a little lighter on the tongue-burning spiciness. We let these wings sit for a good long while in our own special marinade and then coat them with a dry rub. The marinade and the dry rub saturate the chicken with a subtle blend of flavors and keep it super juicy and almost fall-apart tender. Our blue cheese dip is the perfect piquant accent to the smokiness of the wings, with just enough bite to stand up to the deep barbecue flavors. This starter is hearty enough to stand on its own when accompanied by a plate of cut vegetables. But be warned: try these little beauties just once, and you'll never settle for plain old Buffalo chicken wings again.

Serves 4

Blue Cheese Dip

2 cups blue cheese crumbles, divided

1 cup mayonnaise

½ cup buttermilk

2 teaspoons hot sauce

1 teaspoon Worcestershire sauce

½ teaspoon kosher salt

¼ cup finely chopped scallions

¼ cup finely chopped celery

Marinade

½ cup vegetable oil

½ cup hot sauce

4 tablespoons Virgil's Dry Rub (page 159)

4 tablespoons granulated garlic

4 tablespoons granulated onion

Juice of ½ lemon

Wings

8 large chicken wings

½ cup Virgil's Dry Rub (page 159)

Sauce

10 tablespoons unsalted butter

1 teaspoon cornstarch

4 tablespoons white vinegar

¾ cup hot sauce

¼ teaspoon cayenne pepper

1. To make the dip, combine 1 cup of the blue cheese, mayonnaise, buttermilk, hot sauce, Worcestershire sauce, and salt in the bowl of a food processor and blend on low until smooth.

2. Remove to a medium mixing bowl and fold in the rest of the blue cheese, scallions, and celery, being sure to break up the larger blue cheese crumbles. Place in a covered container and refrigerate overnight.

3. Mix all the marinade ingredients in a large mixing bowl. Place the wings in a large container with a lid and pour the mixture over the wings. Toss until the wings are thoroughly coated. Cover and refrigerate for 2 days.

4. Preheat the grill or smoker to 245°F.

5. Spread out the wings on a sheet pan and wipe away any excess marinade. Sprinkle liberally with the dry rub, coating the wings all over.

6. Position the wings on the grill away from the direct heat of the coals or burners, and add hickory to the smoker, or hickory chips on the coals or gas burners.

7. Cook the wings for about 3 hours, flipping every 30 minutes (their internal temperature should be about 165°F when cooked).

8. While the wings are cooking, cut the butter for the sauce into 1-inch cubes and refrigerate. Whisk the cornstarch into the white vinegar, in a small bowl.

9. In a medium sauté pan over medium heat, bring the hot sauce to a simmer and whisk in the thickened vinegar. Return to a simmer, cook for 1 minute, and remove from the heat.

10. Add the cayenne and slowly whisk in the cold butter. Keep warm until serving.

11. Remove the wings from the smoker or grill and put half of them into a bowl, cover with the sauce, and toss. Repeat with the remaining wings and serve on a platter, with the blue cheese dip on the side.

THE RIGHT BEER: A slightly bitter or tart beer works best with the strong dry rub and smoky flavors of these wings. Styles such as amber, farmhouse ale, or ESB (extra special bitter) work best with this recipe. We serve our wings with Goose Island Sofie (Belgian-style ale), Stoudt's Scarlet Lady Ale E.S.B., Dixie Blackened Voodoo Lager, Abita Amber, Brooklyn Pennant Ale '55 (pale ale), and Magic Hat #9.

 ★ Virgil's BBQ Tip ★

Depending on what type of grill you're using, it may be a bit of a battle to keep the temperature down to an average of 245°F. If the temperature just won't settle below 300°F to 350°F, reduce the cooking time for the wings to about an hour.

Outrageous Barbecued Nachos

Mexican cowboys known as *vaqueros* brought their own brand of barbecue into Texas. They called it *barbacoa*, and it was only natural that they'd bring other dishes from home to round out their slow-cooked cow heads. That's how salsa came to be common on cookout tables across the country, and why nachos are just as much an American crowd pleaser as they are a Mexican standard. Our barbecued nachos give us a chance to use up any extra barbecue we have from the main course, which is why we incorporate three types of meat. For your purposes, no harm done if you decide to use just one type of beef, chicken, or pork—but it has to be barbecued, and preferably pulled. No matter what barbecue you include, this much is sure: these nachos are quick and easy to make, and will thrill cookout guests or your family. They are to regular nachos what steak is to hamburger. The little ones go especially crazy for these; kids will tuck into these like nobody's business.

Serves 4–6

3 ounces (about 1 cup) pulled pork (page 215)

3 ounces (about 1 cup) pulled chicken (page 229)

3 ounces (about 3 slices) sliced and chopped barbecued brisket (page 171)

1½ cups Virgil's Mild BBQ Sauce (or substitute your favorite mild barbecue sauce)

¾ (10-ounce) bag tortilla chips

1 cup shredded Monterey Jack cheese

1 cup shredded mild cheddar cheese

15 pickled jalapeño slices

1. Preheat the oven to 400°F.

2. Combine the meats and barbecue sauce in a small saucepan over medium heat.

3. Spread half of the tortilla chips on a small cookie sheet. Cover the chips with half of the meat and sauce. Top with half of each cheese.

4. Repeat the process on top of this layer, using the other half of the ingredients.

5. Bake until the cheese is completely melted, about 10 minutes. Remove and top with the jalapeños.

THE RIGHT BEER: You'll want a beer with crisp, clean flavors and enough body to take the heat from the jalapeños and sweetness from the barbecue sauce in these nachos. You can go a couple of different ways here. You may choose a lager to kick up the heat, or go with a richer beer like Mad River Jamaica Red Ale, Shipyard Old Thumper Extra Special Ale (English bitter), or Dixie Blackened Voodoo Lager, all of which will play down the heat.

Trash Ribs

The cardinal sin of barbecue is letting anything go to waste. When a pitmaster makes more ribs than he can serve at a cookout, he can come up with some mighty resourceful (and tasty) ways to take care of the excess. The original trash ribs were just the end trimmings left over from butchering spareribs, but our version is a bit heartier. Because cold ribs don't retain the flavor of ribs just off the grill, this is a great way to put the meat to good use when you've cooked more than the folks at your cookout could eat. Our trash ribs are basically small bites with a big flavor, pairing a touch of sweet fruit with a bit of peppery fire. It's a heck of a combination. These are the perfect starter for giving your tongue a lot to think about while still leaving some room in the stomach for the main course. Word of caution, though: your ribs must be completely chilled before you start working with them, and you'll need a real, honest-to-goodness, heavy cleaver to get the job done (which only adds to the fun of preparing the dish).

Serves 4–6

6 cool, leftover barbecued spareribs

2 cups Virgil's Mild BBQ Sauce (or substitute your favorite mild barbecue sauce)

1 cup Virgil's Apricot BBQ Sauce (page 55)

½ teaspoon cayenne pepper

1. Preheat the oven to 350°F.

2. Separate the rib racks into individual ribs by slicing between the bones. Chop each rib into 2 to 3 equal pieces using a cleaver. Each piece should be about 2 inches long.

3. Spread the pieces on a small sheet pan and bake for about 15 minutes.

4. While the ribs are baking, combine the barbecue sauces and cayenne in a small pot, and bring to a boil.

5. When the rib pieces are browned and have rendered a small amount of their fat, transfer to a large mixing bowl and add 2 cups of the sauce.

6. Toss the ribs and serve on a platter. Divide the remaining sauce into 4 to 6 ramekins or small bowls to use as dip.

Virgil's Apricot BBQ Sauce

1½ tablespoons canola oil

½ cup sliced red onion

2 ounces (about 8) dried apricots

2½ cups Virgil's Mild BBQ Sauce (or substitute your favorite mild barbecue sauce)

¼ cup pineapple juice

½ cup apple juice

½ teaspoon kosher salt

1. Heat the oil in a heavy pot over medium heat, and add the red onion. Cook for 1 minute. Add the apricots and sauté until tender, about 3 minutes.

2. Add the barbecue sauce, fruit juices and salt, and simmer for 20 minutes.

3. Remove from the stove and puree with an immersion blender or in a food processor. This recipe makes about 3 cups. You can use any leftover sauce on chicken, pork, or even as an interesting pasta sauce.

 **THE RIGHT BEER:** This calls for a beer with a body and richness to match up with the sweet sauce that the ribs are cooked in. Browns, ambers, and stouts will all work well. We serve Left Hand Milk Stout, Captain Lawrence Brown Bird Ale, and Rogue Hazelnut Brown Nectar with our trash ribs.

Oh-My-Gosh Jalapeños Rellenos

We're not going to kid you, this starter is a fair bit of work. But we guarantee that the first bite is all it will take to convince you that the dish is well worth the effort. Matter of fact, we've considered calling these "disappearing shrimp" because they never get a chance to go cold when we set them on a table in one of our restaurants. At the heart of these mouthwatering delicacies is the natural marriage between shrimp and hot peppers of any kind. The jalapeño in this dish just seems perfectly suited to the natural sweetness of the grilled shrimp, and they balance each other to make wonderful music on your tongue. They bring big flavor, but aren't filling, which is another reason why they are such a popular starter for bigger barbecue meals. And that same reason makes them ideal as party snacks or game-day quick bites. They are also perfect partners to a homemade pico de gallo or guacamole.

Serves 6

5 jalapeño peppers

6 ounces cream cheese

5 ounces shredded sharp cheddar cheese

5 ounces shredded Monterey Jack cheese

15 jumbo shrimp, peeled and deveined

1 teaspoon kosher salt

1 teaspoon cracked black pepper

6 tablespoons all-purpose flour

6 tablespoons yellow cornmeal

2 large eggs, beaten

3½ cups Panko bread crumbs

1 cup vegetable or soy oil

1. Roast, peel, and split the jalapeños in half and remove the seeds (see Virgil's Kitchen Tips on page 59 for advice on roasting peppers).

2. In a mixing bowl, combine the cream cheese with the two shredded cheeses, and thoroughly mix together.

3. Place the shrimp on a clean flat surface. With a sharp paring knife, gently butterfly each shrimp, cover with a sheet of plastic wrap, and gently pound flat. Season with the salt and pepper.

4. Place one-third of a roasted jalapeño cut lengthwise on top of each shrimp. Form a small amount of the cheese mixture into a tiny football and place on top of the jalapeño. Press together firmly.

5. Set up three small mixing bowls and a small parchment-covered sheet pan. Mix the flour and cornmeal together in the first bowl, the beaten eggs in the second bowl, and the bread crumbs in a third bowl.

6. Lightly dust each shrimp in the flour mix, then dredge in the egg wash and press evenly into the bread crumbs to completely cover the shrimp. As you finish each, place it on the sheet pan. When all the rellenos are done, wrap the pan with plastic and refrigerate for an hour or two (or freeze and fry frozen).

7. When you're ready to serve, place about 1 inch of oil in a deep sauté pan. Heat to 350°F and fry the rellenos for 1 to 1½ minutes on each side.

8. When golden brown, transfer to a plate covered with a few layers of paper towels and blot dry. Serve immediately.

THE RIGHT BEER: This intriguing dish goes best with a tart, fruity beer. A lager or cider will work well with the spicy heat of the jalapeño. We recommend Angry Orchard Hard Cider or Brooklyn Summer Ale.

Virgil's Kitchen Tips

As you can imagine, everybody in the kitchen at Virgil's handles hot peppers quite a bit, so we've learned a habit you should put in practice whenever you deal with raw jalapeños or other hot peppers. Always wash your hands as soon as you're done handling the peppers. You touch your eyes and lips much more than you realize, and a little bit of jalapeño juice can lay a big bit of hurt on an unprotected eyeball, lip, or the lining of the nose.

Grilled Vegetable Salad

Even people who aren't salad eaters (you know who you are) dive into this salad, because it's got that soul-satisfying grilled flavor. This is another Virgil's favorite that you can customize to suit your own preferences—or to adjust for finicky eaters in the family. Grill different vegetables like artichoke hearts, eggplant, onions, or whatever you prefer, and substitute for any that don't appeal to your guests or your family. You can also make this into a filling main dish, using the recipe for one or two salads instead of four, or by adding grilled chicken, or grilled or steamed fish. Either way, this salad is so delicious that people just pretty much forget it's healthy.

Serves 4

1 large yellow squash, ends trimmed, halved lengthwise

2 medium zucchini, ends trimmed, halved lengthwise

4 portobello mushrooms, cleaned, stems removed

8 spears asparagus, ends trimmed

2 small red bell peppers, halved and seeded

¾ cup olive oil, divided

1 teaspoon kosher salt, divided

1 teaspoon cracked black pepper, divided

¼ cup lemon juice

2 small heads iceberg lettuce, cored and coarsely chopped

1 small bunch arugula

1 small bunch watercress

4 plum tomatoes, quartered lengthwise

1 medium cucumber, cut into ½-inch-thick slices

1 cup shredded cheddar cheese

1 cup crumbled blue cheese

1 cup Kalamata olives

1 cup grated carrots, divided

1. Preheat the grill to medium heat. Lightly coat the squash, zucchini, mushrooms, asparagus, and bell peppers with about ¼ cup of oil and season liberally with salt and pepper. Grill until tender and very slightly charred, about 5 minutes per side. Let cool.

2. Thoroughly mix the oil, lemon juice, and a pinch of salt and pepper in a small bowl.

3. Chop the grilled vegetables into ¾-inch pieces. Combine with the rest of the ingredients in a large salad or mixing bowl, reserving a small amount of the carrots.

4. Serve with dressing on the side and the reserved carrots sprinkled on top of the salad.

Grilled Chicken Caesar Salad

This is the Virgil's East Coast, Times Square spin on a classic salad invented by San Diego restaurant owner Caesar Cardini. The original version was as simple as could be, so that it could be prepared with a little bit of showmanship tableside by waiters who weren't necessarily cooks. We've kept the simplicity but ramped up the heartiness factor a bit by adding the always popular topping of grilled chicken, as well as a little extra spice in the dressing. The simple goodness of the chicken is the ideal backdrop to the just-salty-enough taste of the dressing and the crunchy romaine lettuce. This is a fantastic stage setter for heartier barbecue fare like a nice barbecued brisket or savory pulled pork. Make a slightly bigger serving for those non–barbecue eaters in the crowd, and you'll have a main course to please everyone at your cookout!

Serves 1–2

Dressing

2 tablespoons chopped garlic

12 anchovy fillets, chopped

1½ tablespoons chopped fresh parsley

2 egg yolks

2 cups olive oil

½ cup grated Romano cheese

3 tablespoons red wine vinegar

1 tablespoon lemon juice

1½ teaspoons Worcestershire sauce

Pinch of cracked black pepper

Chicken

1 large chicken breast

1 tablespoon vegetable oil

Pinch of kosher salt

Pinch of cracked black pepper

Salad

1 large or 2 small heads romaine lettuce, coarsely chopped

1 cup seasoned "Texas Toast" croutons

1 cup crumbled tortilla chips

½ cup Roasted Red Pepper and Corn Salsa (see "The Salsa Story," page 66), or use your favorite variety of salsa

¼ cup thinly sliced red onion

¼ cup grated Romano cheese, divided

Pinch of kosher salt

Pinch of cracked black pepper

1. Combine the dressing ingredients, except for the olive oil, in a large nonreactive bowl. Blend with an immersion blender, while very slowly pouring in the olive oil in a steady stream. Blend just until all the ingredients are blended into a uniform dressing.

2. Coat the chicken breast in vegetable oil and sprinkle with salt and pepper, and cook on a grill set to medium-high heat. Grill for 10 to 12 minutes per side, until no pink meat remains and the juices run clear (165°F). Let cool and slice.

3. Combine the salad ingredients and chicken in a large salad bowl (reserving a small amount of the cheese) and toss to mix. Drizzle with the dressing and toss again.

4. Serve on chilled salad plates and dust with the remaining cheese.

Backcountry Cobb Salad

As just plain filling and down to earth as it is, the original Cobb salad has a real pedigree. It was invented by the owner of the highbrow Brown Derby restaurant, which was Tinseltown's place to eat and be seen in the golden age of Hollywood. The story goes that the owner was hungry one night and basically threw together a salad using everything he could find in the refrigerator. We put a Southern spin on this West Coast classic with some barbecued and grilled additions, but it's every bit as tasty and satisfying as the original. It can essentially be an all-in-one meal when you don't want multiple courses cluttering up your dinner table, or it can be broken down into multiple servings to please several guests at a cookout. In any case, unlike at the Brown Derby, nobody's going to need to wait for a seat around the picnic table. No reservations, no waiting, and no hungry people at your cookout!

Serves 1–2

1 small head iceberg lettuce, cored and coarsely chopped

½ cup arugula

2 tablespoons watercress

1 cup coarsely diced smoked turkey

5–6 large grilled shrimp (page 255)

2 hard-boiled eggs

5 slices bacon, cooked crisp, chopped

½ avocado, peeled and sliced

2 tablespoons crumbled blue cheese

5 cherry tomatoes, halved

¼ cup Kalamata olives

½ cup Thousand Island dressing (see "A Memorable Condiment," page 72, for Virgil's version)

1. Clean the iceberg lettuce, arugula, and watercress, discarding any wilted or brown leaves or stems. Thoroughly dry and gently mix the greens together in a large salad or mixing bowl.

2. Toss the greens and top with the remaining ingredients, except for the dressing, in the order shown. Arrange the toppings for an appealing presentation.

3. Serve with the dressing on the side.

 The Salsa Story

Salsa may seem like a pretty down-to-earth condiment, but it traces its roots back to the ancient Mayans, Aztecs, and Incas. The concoction lends itself to variations, and earlier Southern barbecues usually featured a house favorite. Salsa has been commercially distributed in the good old U.S. of A. since the 1930s, but we still like whipping up our own. Here's our recipe, but feel free to add and subtract to make it your own. We won't mind.

Virgil's Roasted Corn and Pepper Salsa

Makes about 2 cups

¾ cup fresh corn kernels (cut off the
    cob)
⅓ cup diced roasted red pepper
3 tablespoons chopped large pitted
    Spanish olives
Juice of ½ lime
1½ tablespoons chopped fresh
    cilantro
1½ tablespoons olive oil
Pinch of kosher salt
Pinch of cracked black pepper

1. Heat a small nonstick sauté pan over high heat and, when the pan is hot, add the corn. Do not move the pan or corn. After 1 minute, toss the corn and cook for another 45 seconds.

2. Remove the corn from the pan and set aside to cool.

3. In a large mixing bowl, combine the remaining ingredients and mix thoroughly. Add the corn and mix it in.

4. Refrigerate the salsa to chill thoroughly before serving.

Savannah Salad with Hot Bacon Dressing

Savannah is a town defined by tidal flats and known for what they call "Low Country boils," the regional version of seafood gumbo. This salad captures the nature of that classic dish with plenty of pork flavoring courtesy of the bacon in the salad and the dressing, and a healthy dose of grilled shrimp. We've added some interesting elements like pecans that give the salad plenty of Southern spark, but the flavors will work at any table where hungry people gather. This salad is rich and hearty as can be, and is one of those perfect barbecue starters that teases the palate with shades of the main-course flavors, while still delivering plenty of satisfaction all on its own.

Serves 1–2

Salad

¼ pound slab bacon, trimmed

⅔ cup pecan halves

1 tablespoon honey

2 tablespoons confectioners' sugar

1 small head iceberg lettuce, cored and coarsely chopped

½ cup arugula

½ cup watercress

⅔ cup crumbled blue cheese

⅔ cup thinly sliced red onions

6 grilled shrimp (page 255)

Pinch of kosher salt

Pinch of cracked black pepper

Hot Bacon Vinaigrette

5 slices smoked bacon

2 tablespoons chopped garlic

1 tablespoon chopped shallots

3 tablespoons chopped scallions

2 tablespoons blue cheese crumbles

3 tablespoons Dijon mustard

½ cup red wine vinegar

1 tablespoon plus 1 teaspoon granulated sugar

½ cup olive oil

½ cup rendered bacon fat

Kosher salt, to taste

Cracked black pepper, to taste

1. Preheat the oven to 325°F.

2. Cut the bacon for the lardons into ¾-inch cubes. Spread on a small sheet pan and bake until browned, at least half the fat has rendered (become liquid), and the bacon is crispy. Retain the bacon fat for the dressing, and let the lardons cool to room temperature.

3. Increase the oven temperature to 350°F.

4. Toast the pecans for 5 minutes. Remove to a small mixing bowl, add the honey, and toss. Remove to a clean mixing bowl, add the confectioners' sugar, and toss until evenly coated.

5. Toss the pecans with the rest of the salad ingredients, except for the lardons and dressing, in a large salad or mixing bowl.

6. Cut the bacon for the dressing into ½-inch pieces and sauté in a medium pan over medium-high heat. When crisp, remove and pat dry and reserve the fat to use with the lardon fat, for the dressing.

7. Add the garlic, shallots, and scallions for the dressing to the same pan and sauté until tender, about 5 minutes.

8. Combine the sautéed vegetables, blue cheese, mustard, vinegar, and sugar in a mixing bowl and blend with an immersion blender (or use a food processor) until smooth.

9. Combine the bacon fat with the olive oil in a measuring cup, and pour in a thin stream into the vegetable mix while blending. Fold in the bacon pieces and add salt and pepper, as desired.

10. Pour the dressing over the salad and toss. Serve the salad garnished with the bacon lardons.

A Memorable Condiment

Just about everyone has memories of Thousand Island dressing from their childhood, and that's what makes it such a special condiment. Well, that and its history. The first known mention of this special salad addition comes from a cookbook published in 1900, but the modern version is credited to a fishing guide's wife who prepared it for clients and named it for the "thousand islands" on the St. Lawrence River between the United States and Canada. Doesn't really matter who first put it on a plate, though; it remains a distinctive, tongue-pleasing taste sensation no matter what's in the salad.

Virgil's Thousand Island Dressing

1⅔ cups mayonnaise

¼ cup chopped celery

3 tablespoons chili sauce

1 tablespoon chopped pimento-stuffed green olives

1 tablespoon chopped bread and butter pickles

1 teaspoon sweet pickle relish

1 tablespoon finely chopped yellow onion

1 teaspoon lemon juice

1 teaspoon chopped fresh parsley

1 hard-boiled egg, chopped

Pinch of kosher salt

Pinch of cracked black pepper

Combine all the ingredients in a large mixing bowl and mix until completely incorporated. Refrigerate for at least 1 hour prior to serving.

Oxtail Soup

You'll find versions of this soup all around the world, but especially throughout Asia, where it's a common family meal. That said, in our minds nothing compares to true Southern oxtail soup. The South's version has been around since before we kicked the British out of the country, and it's got a nice little bit of kick and a satisfying dose of beef. The meat is roasted and braised a good long time, which brings out the sweetness in the beef, and makes the vegetables just perfect. All in all, this is one substantial soup that is perfect for setting the stage for a barbecued main course. But, like many cookout starters, you can turn to this recipe as a one-dish meal and a real warm-me-up on cold nights. It freezes well, so don't be afraid to make a big batch for now *and* later.

Serves 6–8

Stock

8 pounds oxtails, fat trimmed and cut into 3-inch-long pieces

½ pound carrots, peeled and coarsely chopped

½ pound celery, coarsely chopped

½ pound yellow onions, peeled and coarsely chopped

¼ cup crushed garlic

½ cup tomato paste

5 dried bay leaves

6 sprigs fresh thyme

Soup

1 cup finely diced ripe tomatoes

3 medium carrots, peeled and finely diced

3 ribs celery, finely diced

½ pound yellow onions, peeled and finely diced

½ cup pearl barley

1 tablespoon kosher salt, plus more for seasoning

½ teaspoon cracked black pepper, plus more for seasoning

1. Preheat the oven to 400°F.

2. Combine the oxtails and stock vegetables in a roasting pan. Roast for 45 minutes.

3. Coat the oxtails and vegetables with the garlic and tomato paste and roast for an additional 20 to 30 minutes, or until brown.

4. Remove the meat and roasted vegetables to a 12-quart stockpot and discard the rendered fat. Add 2 gallons cold water, the bay leaves, and thyme to the pot. Simmer for 3 hours.

5. Remove the oxtails and cool on a sheet pan. When completely cool, remove all of the usable meat from the bones. Refrigerate the meat, discard the gristle, and return the bones to the pot. Simmer for an additional 2 hours.

6. Strain the stock into a clean pot, discarding the bones and vegetables. You should have approximately 1 gallon of beef stock. Add the soup ingredients and bring to a simmer on the stove.

7. Simmer until the barley is tender and the stock reduces by about one-quarter.

8. Dice the oxtail meat and add to the soup. Taste and season with more salt and pepper, as desired, and serve.

Black Bean Soup

Beans have been part of Southern barbecues since before barbecue was knee high to a grasshopper. Truth is, beans are easy to prepare, delicious and filling, go well with all kinds of spices, and don't need refrigeration. They're also pretty healthy, but it's the silky flavor of the black beans in this soup that makes most folks stand up and take notice. Black beans make for a pretty rich and flavorful soup, one that is just right to lay the groundwork for the barbecue to come, with different but compatible flavors. We include Spanish chorizo in ours—dried sausage with an inviting blend of spices. It has to be Spanish—Mexican and Portuguese chorizo and Southern smoked sausage are all well and good in their own right, but entirely different.

Serves 4–5

1½ (16-ounce) bags dried black beans

8–10 slices smoked bacon, diced

5 ribs celery, diced

1 medium yellow onion, diced

10 ounces Spanish chorizo, diced

1 tablespoon dried epazote

1½ teaspoons fresh thyme leaves

½ cup fresh cilantro, divided

1 tablespoon chopped garlic

1 teaspoon ground cumin

3 dried bay leaves

1 tablespoon kosher salt

¼ teaspoon cracked black pepper

4½ quarts (18 cups) chicken stock

1. Soak the beans in 8 cups cold water for 6 hours.

2. In a 6-quart pot over medium-high heat, cook the bacon until crisp.

3. Add the celery and onion and sauté for 3 to 4 minutes. Add the chorizo, epazote, thyme, half the cilantro, garlic, cumin, bay leaves, salt, and pepper. Continue cooking until the mixture is slightly browned.

4. Add the chicken stock and drained beans. Bring to a boil, then reduce the heat and simmer for 60 to 90 minutes, or until the beans are tender and the flavors have melded. Remove from the heat.

5. Use an immersion blender, or a regular blender, to gently pulse the soup so that it is blended but still chunky. (Blend it longer if you prefer a smooth soup texture.) Fold the remaining cilantro into the soup. Garnish with pico de gallo, sour cream, and fried tortilla chips.

3

Drinks

Barbecuing is thirsty work, and not just for the hearty soul who's tending the fire. Sure, you'll gather a proper sweat tending that grill, but all your cookout guests are bound to be feeling the effects of sitting under a summer sun waiting for the delicious main course to come their way. And that's not to mention the barbecue itself; all those blended spices and combinations of sweet and acidic can lead to a mighty urgent thirst. The right refreshment never did any damage to a barbecue cookout.

We've started this chapter out with a couple nonalcoholic classics that are perfect for rehydrating the pitmaster (and for the children in the crowd). Of course, these are tongue-pleasing drinks, so if you or any of your guests is the designated driver, check out our Front Porch Lemonade (page 83) or Pitmaster's Black Sweet Tea (page 84). These both have long histories as crowd favorites at Southern Sunday socials and fun family gatherings alike. And take it from us, kids go crazy for either one of these. We can't seem to get these drinks on the table quick enough for the young ones that visit Virgil's restaurants.

When it comes to more adult beverages, the one that people naturally think of when they think of barbecue is beer. To be sure, beer and barbecue go together like peanut butter and jelly, two partners who are even better as a pair than they are apart. That's why we've included suggestions for perfect pairings of particular beers with the barbecued and grilled recipes throughout this book, and why you'll find some more general advice in "The Road Trip Barbecue and Beer Guide" on page 105. But when all is said and done, you know what beer you like and what barbecue you like, so there isn't really a bad pairing to be had.

Truly, beer is a pretty darn perfect drink for barbecue, but it is by no means the only option. There are a slew of hot-weather drinks that work perfectly with the many flavors of slow-cooked barbecue or quick-seared grilled favorites. The beauty of these drinks is that they aren't just for cookouts. You can serve them up as wonderful mood setters at just about any party, and they can even make a weeknight dinner or movie night a special affair.

We've included here our own twists on some time-tested summer classics like

the Royal Patrón Margarita (page 93) and the To-Die-For Daiquiri (page 103), but we've also thrown in some of our customer favorites that feature more unusual flavor blends—such as The June Bug (page

The right cocktail can add a wonderful element to the powerful flavors of traditional barbecue.

99). Just keep in mind while you're mixing up these recipes that experimentation is all part of the fun. You can try different flavors and play with the measurements to make the drink less—or more—powerful.

★ Virgil's Gear Tip ★

Measuring out drink ingredients is a little bit different than measuring for kitchen recipes. An ounce is really two tablespoons if you want to go at it like that, but you can make it even easier on yourself by picking up a jigger. This bar tool is shaped like an hourglass, with a standard shot measure (1½ ounces) on one end and a 1-ounce measure on the other.

★ Virgil's Bartending Tip ★

When you make as many drinks as we do in our Times Square restaurant, you get pretty good at it, and mistakes are few and far between. But for the inexperienced home bartender, we suggest adding all the non-alcoholic elements first. That way, if you overpour an ingredient or accidentally add the wrong thing, you won't be losing expensive alcohol in a ruined drink.

Front Porch Lemonade

The best barbecue slows down the clock and takes you on a journey down memory lane, to a quieter time and place. So does the right refreshment, and no drink is better suited for that particular trip than a pure and simple, slightly sweetened lemonade. This is the classic cooler for hot days and hot barbecuing alike. The tartness of the lemon juice cuts the sweetness of the syrup just enough so that the drink perks you up without puckering your face. Always use fresh lemons for your lemonade, and if you want to mix things up a little bit, try using the lemon-orange hybrid known as a Meyer lemon (they aren't available everywhere in the country, but if you can find them, they're an interesting combination of sweet and tart citrus flavors). Quadruple the recipe to make a pitcher, 'cause after that first sip you're going to want more than one glass—and that's a Virgil's guarantee.

Serves 1

2 ounces simple syrup (see Virgil's Bartending Tip, below)

1½ ounces fresh-squeezed lemon juice

1. Combine the syrup and lemon juice with 3½ ounces cold water in a cocktail shaker (or pitcher, if increasing the quantity) and stir vigorously.

2. Serve over ice in a tall glass.

 Virgil's Bartending Tip

Simple Syrup is a standard ingredient in many different drinks, and could hardly be easier to make. Heat equal parts water and sugar over medium heat, until the sugar is entirely melted. Let the mixture cool and refrigerate until you need it.

Pitmaster's Black Sweet Tea

Back in the late 1800s, this was a Southern drink of luxury, known as a display of wealth because it featured both hard-to-get black tea and copious amounts of precious, expensive sugar (the first recorded recipe was published in the magazine *Housekeeping in Old Virginia* in 1879). Although it has become more affordable to make, this drink has remained one of the most popular in the South for that hit-the-spot, thirst-quenching sweetness. You might want to dial back on the sugar a bit, but we recommend you think twice—the sweetness is the whole darn point. It's just about the perfect refreshment for a sweltering summer day or working over a grill going full blazes.

Serves 4

12 bags black tea

2 cups granulated sugar

5 slices fresh lemon

4 lemon wedges, for garnish

1. Toss the tea bags into a large, heat-proof pitcher and cover with 2 quarts boiling water.

2. Add the sugar and lemon, and let steep for one hour. Remove the tea bags and lemon slices after the tea is brewed.

3. After the tea is completely cool, add 2 quarts cold water and refrigerate. Serve in tall glasses filled with ice, garnished with lemon wedges.

Georgia Peach Tea

This is the South's answer to the classic Long Island Iced Tea, and it is ruled by the flavor of the Peach State's most hallowed fruit, a luscious, sweet, natural flavor that finds its way into many Southern barbecue marinades. The peach flavor perfectly balances the acidity of the tea and bite of the citrus in this drink. The combination of a bit of tang and some sugary fruit goodness makes this a beverage that can quench the most powerful of thirsts and will hold up well to your favorite barbecue. This is a favorite among big parties at Virgil's, and we suggest you consider serving it at your next big family celebration or holiday affair.

Serves 4

1 cup Absolut Citron vodka

1 cup Absolut Wild Tea vodka

½ cup peach schnapps

3 cups Front Porch Lemonade (page 83)

1 cup iced tea

4 lemon wheels, for garnish

1. Fill a large pitcher with ice. Combine all the liquid ingredients in the pitcher and stir.

2. Serve in tall glasses filled with ice and garnish with lemon wheels.

Makers Mark Mint Julep

Few drinks can boast the pedigree and distinctive flavors of a mint julep, and no mint julep tastes as good as one made with the premium bourbon Makers Mark. At Virgil's, we make our juleps with this genteel, smooth, and smoky sipping bourbon because it's the perfect partner for the strong dose of mint. This beautiful beverage is the drink of choice for the hoity-toity crowd that sits in the boxes at Churchill Downs to watch the running of the Kentucky Derby. But don't you be fooled—this invigorating concoction is just as at home in your backyard, served alongside your best barbecue. This cocktail is one of a group called "smashes," involving ingredients that are muddled (crushed) to get to their very essence. The process makes for a refreshing and powerful drink that's just perfect as a complement to true slow-cooked barbecue with its char and smoked flavors. Mint juleps are celebration drinks, which is why this recipe makes a party-sized quantity. Trust us; there won't be any left over.

Makes about 15 drinks

1 bunch mint, sprigs reserved for garnish

1 (1-liter) bottle Maker's Mark bourbon whisky

1½ cups Simple Syrup (see Virgil's Bartending Tip on page 85)

1 tablespoon powdered sugar, for garnish

1. Chop up most of the mint, reserving sprigs for garnish, and add to the bottle of bourbon. Steep with the top on for 24 hours, and then strain out the mint.

2. Thoroughly mix the infused bourbon with the Simple Syrup in a large pitcher. Pour into tall glasses filled with crushed ice. Garnish each drink with a mint sprig and a sprinkle of the powdered sugar, and serve.

Virgil's Bartending Tip

Crushed ice is not always easy to find, but you can easily make your own. Securely wrap up a couple glassfuls of cube ice in a sturdy, clean cotton towel, and place the towel on a cutting board or other surface that won't be damaged by a few mean blows. Then hit the ice with a wooden mallet or meat tenderizer until the ice is completely crushed.

The Hurricane

There are lots of different versions of the Hurricane, but all trade on the sweetness of rum combined in a fruity blend that disguises the alcohol. That's because the hurricane was invented by a bar owner who needed to get rid of some less-than-perfect rum back in the day. These days, we create our Hurricanes with high-quality dark rum that adds a bit of depth and complexity—and a hint of heavy molasses—to an otherwise light and fruity drink. A sugary fruit drink like this is sure to go down mighty smooth on a hot day. It's also the perfect drink with heavier barbecued foods like brisket, or anything cooked especially spicy. Or just as a poolside beverage to make those tanning hours go a bit quicker.

Serves 1

1 ounce light rum

1 ounce dark rum

1½ ounces passion fruit juice or puree

1 ounce orange juice

2 ounces Simple Syrup (see Virgil's Bartending Tip on page 85)

½ ounce grenadine

1 slice of orange, for garnish

1 maraschino cherry, for garnish

1. Combine all the liquid ingredients in a cocktail shaker filled with ice. Shake vigorously for several seconds.

2. Pour into a hurricane glass (shaped like an upside-down bell) or a pint glass filled with ice. Garnish with an orange slice and a cherry.

The Royal Patrón Margarita

Barbecue has a lot to thank Mexico for: the habañero pepper, slow-cooked cow heads, spicy salsas, and—the import to end all imports—the margarita. The secret to this Virgil's favorite is the top-shelf tequila we use. A premium silver tequila has a clean finish with no aftertaste, providing a smooth base to this drink that even non–tequila lovers will like. We also use fresh lime juice instead of the bottled stuff, to give the drink a fresher quality and a bit more citrus bite. By adding Cointreau instead of the standard triple sec, we give our version a nice rounded floral finish that makes this one a perfect beverage for hot summer cookouts. Viva la margarita!

Serves 1

Coarse sea salt

1 lime wedge

2 ounces Patrón Silver tequila

1 ounce fresh lime juice

1 ounce Simple Syrup (see Virgil's
    Bartending Tip on page 85)

Dash of Cointreau

Splash of orange juice

1 lime wheel, for garnish

1. Fill a shallow saucer with coarse sea salt. Wipe a lime wedge around the rim of a margarita or pint glass and then dip and twist the glass, rim down, in the salt. (Skip this step if you prefer your margaritas salt-free.) Carefully fill the glass with ice, leaving the salted rim intact.

2. Fill a cocktail shaker three-quarters full of ice and pour all the liquid ingredients into the shaker. Shake for five seconds.

3. Carefully pour the drink into the glass and garnish with a lime wheel.

Fresh Watermelon 'Rita

At Virgil's we love to put our own unique spin on summertime classics, and what better way to improve an already great drink than with the King of Summer Fruits? Adding watermelon to a margarita creates a natural marriage between the refreshing sweetness of the watermelon and the sharper flavors of the tequila and lime juice. It also creates an unusual drink that will add some stunning color to your cookout table. If you fall in love with this drink and think you might want to make it when the melon is out of season, cut the watermelon chunks and freeze them in ice cube trays—the frozen cubes can be thawed and muddled as needed. You can also serve these at a festive party in the melon punch bowl described on page 96.

Serves 1

2 chunks watermelon (each the size of your thumb)

2 ounces silver tequila

1 ounce fresh lime juice

1 ounce Simple Syrup (see Virgil's Bartending Tip on page 85)

Dash of Cointreau

Coarse sea salt (optional)

1 watermelon wedge, for garnish

1. Crush the watermelon in the bottom of a pint glass with a shaker top. Fill the glass with ice and add the liquid ingredients. Shake vigorously for 5 to 10 seconds.

2. Strain into another pint or margarita glass filled with ice (salt the rim first, if desired, as described on page 91). Garnish with a small watermelon wedge.

★ The Watering Whole ★

Sometimes you just want to go the extra mile to turn special meals into special events. Times like that, you can make a splash with your beverages by serving them up in a "watermelon punch bowl." Cut a third off the end of a watermelon and scoop out the insides of the larger section, using a melon baller or a small ice cream scoop. (Save the watermelon for fruit salad or to use in our Fresh Watermelon 'Rita on page 93!) Cut a very thin slice off the bottom of your punch bowl so that it stands up stable on the table and—if you want to get a bit fancy—cut the top edge into teeth or curves or whatever shape you like. Then fill the bowl with the refreshment of your choice for a super-thirst-quenching presentation. Kids get a big kick out of this creation, especially if you let them participate in making the bowl (they can even doodle designs in the side with a small spoon or the melon baller).

The Texas Gringo

When the temperature regularly heads north of a hundred degrees in the shade, it pays to know how to cool off. That's why smart Texans turn to this fine beverage. This is a Longhorn State version of the classic margarita, with the cleaner finish of a distinctive, handmade Texas vodka replacing the heavier traditional tequila. Two kinds of citrus provide an extra refreshing tartness and balance the sweeter parts of the mix. No matter how powerful your thirst is, the Texas Gringo will cut it down to size, and give you a nice mellow feeling to boot.

Serves 1

2 ounces Tito's Handmade Vodka

1 ounce fresh-squeezed lime juice

1 ounce orange juice

1 ounce Simple Syrup (see Virgil's Bartending Tip on page 85)

Dash of Cointreau

1 lime wedge, for garnish

1. Combine the liquid ingredients in a cocktail shaker and shake vigorously for 5 to 10 seconds.

2. Pour into a pint glass filled with ice. Serve garnished with a wedge of lime.

The Mint-Perfect Blueberry Mojito

This is a special drink for special occasions. The mojito was Ernest Hemingway's second favorite hot-weather cocktail next to the daiquiri, and the man knew his cocktails. The mint in a standard mojito serves up a refreshing bite that just seems to cool down the hottest days and the hottest food. Virgil's bartenders put a twist on the traditional flavors by adding some blueberry. Mint and blueberry maybe aren't the first combination you would think up for a drink, but when it comes to the Virgil's bar, we never shy away from exploring new flavor combinations—and this is one of our best. It's a bright treat for the tongue and just as much a treat for the eye, and it offers the perfect counterpoint to heavier barbecued foods, such as brisket and pulled pork with tomato-based sauces.

Serves 1

5 small blueberries

3 lime wedges

1 large sprig mint, with a small portion reserved for garnish

½ ounce blueberry syrup

2 ounces light rum

Splash of Sprite

1. Muddle the first four ingredients together in a highball glass (reserving a small sprig of mint for garnish). Pour the rum into the glass.

2. Fill the glass with ice, top with a shaker, and shake for several seconds.

3. Top with the Sprite and serve garnished with the sprig of mint.

The June Bug

Here's another pretty little party pick-me-up that Virgil's customers just seem to love. It's a beautiful, delicious drink named for a not-so-beautiful and (we're pretty sure) not-so-delicious beetle. This drink's roots are in the tropics, where it has slaked many a heated thirst. The beverage is a blend of clean, fruit tastes and melon liqueur that is given a bit more oomph with some handcrafted Texas vodka. This is one unique cocktail and, as one bartender in our Time Square restaurant puts it, "it drinks velvety." That means it goes down smooth and easy. Try it paired with grilled fish, veggies, or lighter pork dishes.

Serves 4

1 cup Tito's Handmade Vodka

1 cup melon liqueur

1 cup rum

2 cups pineapple juice

¼ cup cold water

Maraschino cherries, for garnish

Fresh pineapple slices, for garnish

1. Mix the liquid ingredients together in a small pitcher. Stir until thoroughly blended.

2. Add ice to the pitcher and stir again. Pour into hurricane glasses or highball glasses filled with ice.

3. Garnish with cherries and pineapple slices, and serve.

The Spicy Habañero

This drink takes its cue from some of the best hot sauces on the market. It's not just the peculiarly intense heat that makes a habañero chili pepper special, this particular chili pepper adds citrus flavors and nice aroma wherever it goes. We put it to work in our own special version of the traditional margarita, one that combines the spiciness of the pepper with a whole lot of tasty and refreshing citrus flavors. The infused tequila is key, because the infusion process keeps the chili pepper's heat from overwhelming the drink. Trust us; you won't find a better beverage for cutting heavy, smoky barbecue flavors, or for adding lots of life to your next cookout party.

Serves 1

Raw sugar

1 lime wedge

2 ounces spiced tequila (see Virgil's Bartending Tip on page 102)

1 ounce triple sec

½ ounce Simple Syrup (see Virgil's Bartending Tip on page 85)

¼ ounce lemon juice

1¼ ounces lime juice

1 ounce Ruby Red grapefruit juice

1. Fill a shallow saucer with raw sugar and run a lime wedge around the rim of a hurricane glass. Twist the rim of the glass in the sugar to thoroughly coat the rim.

2. Combine the liquid ingredients in a shaker glass full of ice. Shake for about 5 seconds.

3. Fill the sugared hurricane glass with ice, being careful not to disturb the rim, and pour in the shaken drink.

Virgil's Bartending Tip

Infusing alcohol can be a fun way to add interesting flavors to your cocktails. Here's how you infuse tequila to make the "spiced tequila" we use in our Spicy Habañero. You can use these same instructions to infuse tequila with other flavors, such as pineapple, red chili peppers, ginger, or whatever taste floats your boat and works with the flavor of the tequila. You can infuse other alcohols such as vodka or rum in the same way. Experiment with mint or cinnamon (use cinnamon sticks) rum, or pomegranate or bacon vodka.

Virgil's Habañero Tequila Infusion

Cut 1 habañero pepper in half and drop it into a 1-liter bottle of premium silver tequila. Allow the tequila to steep for at least one day before using, and leave the pepper in the bottle.

To-Die-For Daiquiri

At Virgil's we like to add a little something extra to almost everything we do. That's how we came up with this version of the classic cocktail. Originally from Cuba, the daiquiri does a lot with a little, because it isn't much more than rum and lime juice. We added a touch of sweet summer fruit and an intriguing bit of bitter for an incredible barbecue refreshment. This combination is refreshing and cooling, so it's a great choice for long, lazy summer afternoons spent gathered around a slow-cooking piece of meat or pork. Lightly sweet and rain-shower refreshing, it's sure to revive guests and pitmaster alike!

Serves 1

Granulated sugar

2 tablespoons chopped fresh strawberries

2 dashes of bitters

2 ounces premium aged rum

1 ounce lime juice

½ ounce Simple Syrup (see Virgil's Bartending Tip on page 85)

1 lime wheel, for garnish

1. Sprinkle a little granulated sugar over the chopped fresh strawberries in the bottom of a shaker glass. Add the bitters and muddle with a wood muddler or the back of a bar spoon.

2. Add the daiquiri ingredients to the glass and shake for several seconds.

3. Strain into a tall glass filled with crushed ice and garnish with a lime wheel.

Virgil's Lemon Drop Martini

Special occasions call for a special drink, so we've included the one we serve with birthday and anniversary barbecues and other memorable get-togethers. This is a cross between a couple of different cocktails, and the result is completely unique and taste-bud tickling. It's an uncomplicated blend of sweet and sour, and a little bit bracing. But this drink is really about the presentation. The fancy glass dusted with sugar is about as eye-catching as a perfectly barbecued brisket, though it takes a whole lot less time to make!

Serves 1

Granulated sugar

1 lemon wedge

2 ounces Tito's Handmade Vodka

¾ ounce lemon juice

1½ ounces Simple Syrup (see Virgil's Bartending Tip on page 85)

1 teaspoon peach liqueur

1 lemon wheel, for garnish

1. Fill a shallow saucer with granulated sugar. Run a lemon wedge around the rim of a martini glass, and press the rim of the glass into the sugar.

2. Shake the vodka, lemon juice, and simple syrup in a shaker filled halfway with ice. Strain the drink into the martini glass without disturbing the sugared rim.

3. Slowly pour the peach liqueur down the inside edge of the glass so that it settles on the bottom. Serve garnished with a lemon wheel.

The Road Trip Barbecue and Beer Guide

Mixed drinks are great for the right occasion, but beer is never wrong for a barbecue feast. Finding the perfect beer for your barbecue is a matter of some rather enjoyable experimentation. Not only are you trying to match up the beer's character against the flavors of the particular food you have on the grates, you'll also want to satisfy your own personal taste preferences. Here are a few suggestions from the beverage experts at Virgil's Time Square restaurant.

✓ **Pulled pork:** Think amber ale or a lager. Lightly roasted or caramelized malts really accent the rich, sweet flavors in most barbecued pork. You might venture into IPA (India Pale Ale) territory, but just make sure you choose one that goes light on the hops. If you like your pulled pork heavy on the sauce, consider a citrus-heavy pale ale.

✓ **Pork ribs:** A lager with a clean finish can clear your palate between servings of sticky, rich ribs, but avoid more bitter versions that would fight the delicate sweetness of the meat. In general, look to choose a beer with dominant malt flavors, preferably something with nice caramel overtones. Classic Bavarian dark lagers work well, as do heavier "black" *saisons* (Belgian farmhouse ales).

✓ **Brisket:** You're going to need a beer that can stand up to the flavors of the char in this beef—especially the distinctive bark on the outside of the barbecued meat. Turn to an Oktoberfest-style amber, or a black lager such as a classic *schwarzbier*.

✓ **Chicken and turkey:** Whether grilled or slow cooked with a dry rub, barbecued fowl is best complemented by a lighter, golden *saison*-style beer. A beer that goes a bit heavy on the citrus and hops will be especially good with barbecued birds.

✓ **Hamburgers:** This simple dish calls for an equally simple, light and refreshing pale ale. Your everyday cookout beer like Budweiser or Pabst is just fine with a well-grilled burger.

✓ **Grilled steak:** Turn to a lush, full-bodied Belgian ale or other malt-heavy brew that can stand up to the strong flavors of the meat.

✓ **Seafood:** Lighter versions such as grilled shrimp call for a wheat beer, or crisp, amber versions of *saison*. A basic lager with a clean finish will also complement fish of all kinds.

★ 4

Sides

Some of the best barbecue joints across the South have a long-standing tradition of throwing in two or three sides with every main course. It's a tradition we at Virgil's heartily endorse. A barbecue cookout is rarely a one-performer show. You want the whole theatrical production—and that's gonna mean side dishes.

The classic barbecue sides are the revered trio of baked beans, potato salad, and coleslaw. Those were always on the table for the Sunday church socials and potluck get-togethers that make up such a big part of barbecue's history throughout the South. Sides in general have always played a part in the "community" character of barbecue, as a food that brings friends and family together. Aunt Mabel would bring her world-famous potato salad, while Susie from down the way would bake a whole mess of her biscuits, and Bob might whip up some of his unique slaw while he was waiting for that pork shoulder to finish smoking. The barbecue was always the centerpiece, but there was also plenty of other food to accommodate every taste, something to satisfy every kind of hunger. It was a nod to all the diverse people this uniquely American cuisine connects us to.

Beyond the social, side dishes are just a great way to make a barbecued main dish even better. They add different—but complementary—flavors and textures to the meal and really round things out. We call it "a meal with all the fixin's," and it's pretty darn popular among the people who crowd around our tables.

Some sides are about "barbecue-izing" vegetables, while others add a pasta or grain to a big protein meal. In any case, we tend to go for the classics. Traditional side dishes like Grandma's Collard Greens (page 112) and Sunday Picnic Deviled Eggs (page 119) are super-delicious standards that have stood the test of time and proven their worth through countless meals. The best sides have a way of appealing

That's how we make our perfectly shaped hush puppies!

to young and old alike, so the whole family is sure to enjoy whatever you put on the table.

We find that it's best to mix up the type of sides you're serving—like putting collard greens with mac and cheese. That way, you're adding a lot of interest to the meal and mixing in a lot of different flavors and textures. Sides are where you can get out of your comfort zone and try whole new types of dishes without risking much. If you find a favorite among the dishes in this chapter, we'd suggest multiplying the recipe so that you have a little for later. Barbecue side dishes just seem to make excellent leftovers, and they can certainly work as great lunches or snacks all on their own.

Of course, our side dishes can wear many other hats as well. They can be main-course options for those rare individuals at your cookout who might not be partial to barbecued meat or fowl. They can also stand in as part of a weeknight indoor meal, or a potluck addition at your next local community get-together. At the end of the day, there is always a place on the table for a well-made tasty side dish.

Grandma's Collard Greens

Barbecue and collard greens just go naturally together, like Flatt and Scruggs. The marriage works so well because collard greens are a sturdy member of the cabbage family, with a dense nutty flavor and firm texture that matches up incredibly well with the spices and smoke in most barbecue. Collard greens are often heavily spiced, but our version is a little tamer; we cook our greens 'til they're nice and tender and the rich, sweet, buttery flavor comes right out. These greens are jam packed with vitamins and minerals—but we're betting you'll be more interested in the subtle blend of ever-so-slightly bitter and salty flavors. (Add hot sauce if you want a little more kick.)

Serves 6–8

½ pound uncooked bacon, diced

2½ pounds collard greens, stems removed

3 cups chicken stock

4 tablespoons white vinegar

2 tablespoons granulated sugar

¼ teaspoon Virgil's Creole Seasoning (page 160)

¼ teaspoon ground white pepper

1. Heat a large saucepan on high heat, and render the bacon until crisp.

2. Add the collard greens and sauté until they begin to wilt. Add the remaining ingredients and lower the heat to a simmer.

3. Simmer the greens until tender, about 30 minutes.

Virgil's Kitchen Tip

The secret to great collard greens starts in the produce aisle. Make sure all the leaves are firm and light green throughout—wilted or yellowed leaves can ruin the whole dish. Collard greens, like all sturdy greens, should be thoroughly washed before use so that you avoid any nasty grit in the finished dish. Fill a clean sink with lukewarm water and dip the greens vigorously into the water, letting any dirt and grit float to the bottom of the sink. Drain and repeat three times, or until the greens are grit-free.

Lip-Smacking Corn Muffins

Add this delicious side dish to the list of things we can thank Native Americans for. In fact, early settlers called the cornmeal at the heart of this treat "Indian meal" because they learned how to make it from the country's original inhabitants. This muffin has become a cookout favorite that serves as the perfect backdrop to the heavier flavors in smoked beef and pork. Recipes for corn muffins spread far and wide—it's even the state muffin of Massachusetts! We mix in a little cheese and a lot of spices in our version, to give this classic the Virgil's signature touch and make the flavors a little more complex. They're traditionally served with butter and honey, but we've created our own maple butter to go with this recipe (you'll find it on page 116). Be careful not to serve these muffins early at your cookout, or people will fill up before they ever get to the main course!

Serves 4–6

1⅓ cups yellow cornmeal

¾ cup all-purpose flour

½ cup, plus 1 tablespoon granulated sugar

1 tablespoon kosher salt

¾ tablespoon baking powder

1 teaspoon baking soda

2 cups buttermilk

½ cup whole milk

2 eggs, beaten

6 tablespoons unsalted butter, melted

½ (8-ounce) bag shredded cheddar cheese

1 cup fresh corn kernels

3 tablespoons chopped scallions

3 tablespoons chopped fresh cilantro

½ teaspoon hot sauce

1. Preheat the oven to 400°F. Butter a muffin tin and dust with flour.

2. Thoroughly combine the first six ingredients in the bowl of a stand mixer or a large mixing bowl, if using a hand mixer. Combine and mix the remaining ingredients in a separate mixing bowl.

3. Slowly add the wet mix to the dry, while blending on low speed. Continue blending until entirely incorporated.

4. Fill each muffin tin three-quarters full of the batter. Bake for 18 to 20 minutes, or until light golden brown on top.

5. Remove the muffin tins from the oven and allow to cool for 15 to 20 minutes. Serve slightly warm, with Virgil's Maple Butter.

Virgil's Maple Butter

Makes about 2 cups

3 sticks unsalted butter, softened

1 cup pure maple syrup

½ teaspoon kosher salt

½ teaspoon Cholula Hot Sauce

In a stand mixer, with a paddle attachment, or using a hand mixer, beat the butter on medium and then on high, until the butter is soft and airy. Add the remaining ingredients and blend until fully incorporated. Refrigerate in a small covered container until ready to use.

Hickory Pit Baked Beans

This dish is simple as pie to make—simpler, in fact. It had to be, because Native Americans and early settlers who first baked the beans in a ceramic bean pot weren't about to fuss with anything that was hard to cook. The idea was to use navy beans and make them as tender as possible. Pork is usually added to the dish to make it a little more substantial, but we add in some of our famous smoked brisket for a much more unique barbecue-style flavor. If you don't happen to have any extra brisket, you can always substitute smoked bacon. Either way, the smoky goodness of this dish is the perfect accent to a hearty barbecued meal. It's also great for just about any other meal, including breakfast—those darn Brits put them right on top of eggs and toast!

Serves 6–8

¾ cup beef broth

½ cup Virgil's Mild BBQ Sauce (or substitute your favorite mild barbecue sauce)

¼ cup molasses

2 tablespoons yellow mustard

¼ cup dark brown sugar

1 tablespoon Virgil's Dry Rub (page 159)

¾ teaspoon liquid smoke

⅓ pound smoked beef brisket (with as much bark as possible)

4 tablespoons finely diced yellow onions

2 tablespoons finely diced green bell peppers

6 cups baked beans

1. Combine all the ingredients in a large saucepan. Stir until thoroughly blended.

2. Bring to a boil, and then reduce to a simmer. Simmer for 45 minutes. Serve hot.

Sunday Picnic Deviled Eggs

Few dishes scream barbecue picnic quite like deviled eggs, and few deviled egg recipes scream delicious like our version. People just love them because the eggs themselves mellow out some of the spicier elements you're likely to find in any barbecue feast. We've kind of reinvented this traditional favorite, adding in a lot of flavors and textures that make it even more of a complement to a barbecued main course. Our deviled eggs are pretty spicy, but the heat is well balanced by the creamier ingredients. We top ours with chorizo, a Spanish sausage that's full of flavor. You can substitute with smoked bacon chopped up and cooked in a pan if you absolutely can't lay your hands on some chorizo.

Serves 4–6

8 extra-large eggs

¼ cup mayonnaise

1 teaspoon Creole mustard

¼ teaspoon Cholula Hot Sauce

¼ teaspoon ground cumin

½ teaspoon kosher salt

¼ teaspoon cracked black pepper

2 teaspoons finely chopped pickled jalapeño slices

1 teaspoon pickled jalapeño juice

½ Hass avocado, peeled and pitted

Pinch of smoked paprika

1 tablespoon chopped fresh cilantro

2 ounces dried Spanish chorizo

1. Place the eggs in a medium pot and cover with cold water. Bring to a boil, cover the pot, and remove from the heat. Keep covered for 11 minutes, then remove the eggs from the water and place in a bowl of ice water to stop the cooking process.

2. Pre-heat a sauté pan. Cut the chorizo into very small dice and saute until crispy, set aside to cool.

3. In a small bowl, combine the mayonnaise, mustard, hot sauce, cumin, salt, pepper, jalapeño, and jalapeño juice.

4. When the eggs have cooled, carefully crack the shells and peel under cold running water. Slice the eggs lengthwise and remove the yolks, being careful to leave the whites intact.

5. Combine the avocado and egg yolks in a small bowl, and mash together with a fork until smooth.

6. Add the avocado mixture to the mayonnaise mixture and blend thoroughly. Spoon the mixture into each half of egg white. Dust with the paprika, sprinkle with the cilantro and chorizo, and serve.

Virgil's Simple Slaw

The wonderful thing about coleslaw is all the many ways it can be made. Talk to any Southerner, and they're bound to have their own opinions about the best slaw recipe. That's because there are about a million recipes around the country. We think ours stands up to any we've tasted on our road trips, and most of the visitors to our restaurants seem to agree—we can't make it fast enough to satisfy the crowds. Our slaw is simple and delicious, made in the traditional way using mayonnaise for a creamy bright dressing that brings out the best in the cabbage. This is also a straightforward recipe, which means you're not going to work very hard for a fantastic side dish that's ideal for any barbecue you're putting on the table. Our secret ingredient is bread-and-butter pickles, but remember, it's a secret.

Serves 4–6

2 small heads green cabbage

¼ cup shredded carrots

½ cup chopped bread-and-butter pickles

½ cup granulated sugar

1 tablespoon apple cider vinegar

¼ teaspoon ground white pepper

½ teaspoon kosher salt

1¼ cups mayonnaise

3 tablespoons yellow mustard

2 teaspoons celery seed

1. Remove the outer leaves of the cabbage, slice into quarters, and remove the core. Rinse the quarters and shake out as much water as possible. Thinly slice the cabbage and then chop.

2. In a large mixing bowl, combine the rest of the ingredients and toss to blend. Add the cabbage and fold in to thoroughly coat. Refrigerate before serving, at least 30 minutes.

Crispy Hush Puppies

Legend has it that way back when, Southern hunters and fishers used to toss these crispy treats to the dogs to keep them quiet during trips to the woods so that the dogs wouldn't bay and scare off the day's dinner. No offense to our canine friends, but we think that's just plumb wasteful. Better to let the hounds bay than lose any of this crunchy goodness and the many subtle flavors hidden inside the fried shell. Traditionally, these are served with grilled and fried fish, but you'll find that they're a filling addition to beef, pork, and chicken barbecue as well. They are also an incredible substitute to anywhere you'd serve bread, and they even make a great snack in between meals.

Serves 4–6

1 cup yellow cornmeal

1 cup all-purpose flour

⅓ cup minced yellow onion

¼ cup fresh corn kernels

½ tablespoon granulated sugar

2 teaspoons onion powder

1 teaspoon baking powder

1½ teaspoons kosher salt

1 cup buttermilk

1 extra-large egg

4 cups canola oil

1. Combine the first eight ingredients in a medium mixing bowl. In a separate bowl, mix together the egg and buttermilk.

2. Add the buttermilk mixture to the dry mixture and blend. Refrigerate for 2 hours.

3. Fill a large and deep sauté pan (or an electric skillet) one-third full of canola oil. Heat to 325°F.

4. Remove the batter from the refrigerator and drop by spoonful into the oil. Fry in batches, being careful not to crowd the pan.

5. Fry for approximately 1½ minutes on each side (or until each side is golden brown). Remove from the oil with a slotted spoon and place on a sheet pan covered with three or four layers of paper towels.

6. When you've fried all the batter and the hush puppies are drained of oil, serve hot with Virgil's Maple Butter (page 116).

Georgia Pecan Rice

There is so much going on in this nutty, chewy, incredibly delicious recipe that it seems a shame to call it a side dish. It would be quite comfortable serving as the main course in a summer meal, but paired with a well-smoked cut of beef or pork, it really shines. The combination of white rice, pecans, and sausage is a hard one to beat, and creates a mix of deep, rich flavors you're not likely to forget anytime soon. This side can hold up to truly spicy barbecue, and food served with sauces, so it's a great addition to any hearty cookout meal you serve.

Serves 4

6 strips of uncooked bacon, diced

1 stick unsalted butter

1½ cups finely diced green bell pepper

1½ cups finely diced scallions

1½ cups finely diced roasted red peppers

¼ pound andouille sausage, diced

3 dried bay leaves

¾ cup pecan pieces

1½ teaspoons kosher salt

¼ teaspoon cracked black pepper

1 pound converted rice

3½ cups hot chicken stock

1. Preheat the oven to 400°F.

2. Heat the bacon in a 4-quart oven-safe pot over medium-high heat until it is almost crispy.

3. Add the butter, green peppers, and scallions and sauté for 3 minutes. Add the red peppers, sausage, bay leaves, pecan, salt, and pepper and continue to sauté for an additional 3 minutes.

4. Add the rice and cook for 3 minutes or until the rice toasts (to seal it prior to cooking and retain plumpness). Add the stock and bring to a boil. Cover and remove to the oven. Bake for about 17 minutes.

5. Remove and check that all the liquid has been absorbed and that the rice is tender. If not, bake for an additional 5 minutes. Uncover and serve hot.

Creole Green Beans

If you want to see simple veggies perk right up, whip up this dish. Although the green beans are the stars, we throw in a big pile of other vegetables to round out the recipe and make it as filling as it looks. It's a wonderful dish for any vegetarians at your cookout, and sure to please salad lovers of every stripe (substitute fresh garden vegetables in season as you or your guests prefer). The herbs and garlic supply a little zip to the beans, but it's really our own Creole seasoning that makes the whole dish sparkle. Our blend of spices gives this side a Louisiana accent, and it makes this one flavor explosion worthy of throwing some beads around in Mardi Gras.

Serves 4–6

4 tablespoons unsalted butter

2½ tablespoons chopped garlic

1 cup thinly sliced red onions

1 cup thinly sliced green peppers

1 cup thinly sliced red peppers

⅔ cup thinly sliced celery

2½ tablespoons Virgil's Creole Seasoning (page 160)

¾ cup chicken stock

½ teaspoon kosher salt

1 (28-ounce) can plum tomatoes, with juice

2 pounds fresh green beans, cleaned and trimmed

4½ tablespoons chopped fresh cilantro

1. Melt the butter in a 2-quart saucepan.

2. Add the garlic, onion, peppers, and celery, and cook until they begin to pick up some color.

3. Add the Creole Seasoning and cook for 2 minutes. Add the stock, salt, and tomatoes. Bring to a boil and then reduce to a simmer.

4. Add the beans and simmer for 15 minutes on low, or until the beans are tender. Add the cilantro and serve.

Crusty Mac and Cheese

We at Virgil's want people to feel comfortable when they come visit us. We don't put on fancy airs and we don't see the point to putting lipstick on a pig. Barbecue is simple, wholesome, filling fare that's best cooked and eaten in comfortable, casual clothes, with a lot of time to spare and good friends nearby. That's why mac and cheese is such an ideal complement to barbecue. It is soul-satisfying creamy goodness for the wonderfully plain moments in life. Sometimes you need some good old comfort food, and no side dish is quite as comforting as mac and cheese. We make ours with just a little spiciness to remind you of where it comes from, and the perfect smoothness of Cheese Wiz. Yes, Cheese Wiz. When something works, we don't worry about what people will think. Like we say, nothing fancy, just belly-pleasing, appetite-solving, gooey goodness.

Serves 4–6

1 pound elbow macaroni

½ teaspoon kosher salt

⅛ teaspoon ground white pepper

½ cup chicken stock

¾ cup heavy cream

½ tablespoon Worcestershire sauce

½ tablespoon hot sauce

½ tablespoon Creole mustard

1¼ cup Cheese Wiz

8 ounces sharp cheddar cheese, shredded

1. Preheat the oven to 350°F. Grease a 2-quart baking dish.

2. Boil the macaroni in a 2-quart saucepan filled with water, until it is *al dente*, or still has some snap when you bite it. Strain the pasta and rinse thoroughly with cold water. Set aside.

3. Combine the remaining ingredients, except for the shredded cheese, in a medium saucepan over medium heat. The mixture should be barely simmering. Whisk periodically. Cook for 7 to 10 minutes.

4. In a large mixing bowl, combine the cheese sauce with the pasta and about one-third of the shredded cheese. Transfer to the baking dish, covering with the remaining shredded cheese, and bake covered for 10 minutes.

5. Uncover and bake for 15 minutes more, or until the top is golden brown.

Southern Accent Cheddar Grits

No true and proud Southerner uses instant grits, and neither should you. We certainly don't. We whip up our grits from scratch, with two different cheeses, some hot sauce, and not much else: you don't *need* much else. These grits make for a truly delicious side that smooths out any hot flavors in your barbecue and will leave your guests asking for seconds. And thirds. Be careful on how you dish these up, though, they're mighty filling. They're also pretty adaptable, and can fit right into just about any weeknight meal you make, whether it comes off the grill or not.

Serves 6–8

6 cups chicken stock

½ pound white stone-ground corn grits

1 stick unsalted butter

¾ pound sharp cheddar cheese, shredded

¼ cup grated Romano cheese

½ teaspoon kosher salt

⅛ teaspoon ground white pepper

1 teaspoon hot sauce

1. Bring the chicken stock to a boil in a large saucepan. Mix in the grits. Reduce the heat to low and cook for about 15 to 20 minutes, stirring occasionally, until the grits are tender but still firm.

2. Add the butter and cheeses and mix until incorporated. Add the salt, pepper, and hot sauce. Taste and adjust the seasonings, as desired, before serving.

Virgil's Barbecue Backstory

Grits are a Southern tradition, and almost 75 percent of the grits sold in America are sold in the South. In fact, the spread from Texas to Virginia is sometimes called the "grit belt," and grits are the official prepared food of Georgia. The rest of the country is learning, though. Thanks to recipes like ours, the Yanks are getting a taste of the real South . . . and if you judge by the smiles at our tables, they're loving it.

Fried Green Tomatoes with Shrimp and Crab Remoulade

This Southern specialty came about when cooks were trying to make good use of the last tomatoes of the season. The idea was to use the tomatoes even if they weren't going to have time to ripen, and what a good idea it was. The traditional way to make these involves a very basic cornmeal crust, but we take ours to a whole 'nother level. We spice up the coating of the tomatoes and then add a mess of shrimp and crab that gives the dish a real bayou feel. This is a fantastic side dish for barbecue beef and pork (which creates a little variety in the meal), but it works equally well as a filling main dish on a noncookout night.

Serves 5

3 cups buttermilk

4 tablespoons Virgil's Creole Seasoning (page 160), divided

2 large green tomatoes, cored and sliced into 10 slices

3 cups Universal Flour (page 167)

1½ to 2 cups canola oil

1 pound Jumbo shrimp, cooked, peeled, and deveined (recommend true Gulf shrimp)

1 pound lump crab meat

1½ cups Virgil's Remoulade (page 40)

1. Combine the buttermilk and Creole Seasoning (reserving about 2 teaspoons) in a large bowl, and mix well. Marinate the tomato slices in the mixture for 10 minutes. Remove the tomatoes and set aside.

2. Set up a dredging station with a bowl containing the Universal Flour, the bowl with the buttermilk mix, and a small sheet pan covered with parchment paper.

3. Dust a tomato slice in the flour mix, shake off the excess, dredge in the buttermilk, and lay on the sheet pan. Repeat with all the remaining slices. Refrigerate until you're ready to serve.

4. Heat about 1 inch of canola oil in a deep saucepan or sauté pan. The oil should be 350°F.

5. Slide the tomatoes one at a time into the oil and fry for 1 to 1½ minutes per side. Fry the tomatoes in batches, being careful not to crowd the pan. When golden brown, transfer to a plate covered with several layers of paper towels and blot dry.

6. To serve, spread the tomato slices on a platter and lightly dust with the remaining Creole Seasoning. Slice the shrimp lengthwise and lay one on each slice. Place a pinch of crab in the middle and cover with 1 to 2 tablespoons of the remoulade. Garnish with more crab and serve.

Good Ol' Mashed Potatoes and Gravy

In the tradition of the best barbecue side dishes, simple mashed potatoes and gravy is just the thing when you want something extra that won't compete with the taste of your barbecue or complicate the meal. This is the very definition of a simple, unfussy side dish. The nice creamy texture and down-to-earth flavors are especially good as a backdrop to really strong barbecue, like a perfectly done barbecued brisket with a sturdy bark on it. Of course, this side is just as appropriate for barbecued chicken or pork. And it makes a good accompaniment on any night that you need a little comfort from your dinner and want something that's easy to make and sticks to your ribs.

Serves 6–8

5 pounds russet potatoes

½ pound unsalted butter, cubed

½ cup heavy cream

1½ cups whole milk

1½ tablespoons kosher salt

½ teaspoon ground white pepper

1. Thoroughly clean and rinse the potatoes. Cut into 1½-inch pieces. Place in a small stockpot and cover with cold water.

2. Bring to a boil, reduce to a simmer, and cook until fork tender—about 15 to 20 minutes. While the potatoes are cooking, make the Country Gravy on page 181.

3. While the potatoes are cooking, combine the butter, cream, milk, salt, and pepper in a saucepan. Bring to a boil and then reduce to keep warm.

4. When the potatoes are tender, drain the water, allow the potatoes to air dry for a minute or two, and mash.

5. Add the cream mixture and incorporate only until smooth. Do not overmix. Serve hot, with the Mushroom Gravy on page 170.

Perfect Buttermilk Biscuits

Biscuits have been around since Americans have been American, but the little beauties we serve at Virgil's couldn't be more different from the hard tack early settlers choked down. In fact, we'll put our rich, pillowy biscuits up against any biscuit anywhere. That's because we make ours with special White Lily Flour and the basic goodness of real butter and buttermilk. Packaged mixes can't even come close to this for pure homespun satisfaction. Our biscuits are the perfect complement to juicy barbecue, especially when you slather them with a little of our very special Virgil's Maple Butter (page 116). You better be ready for big fame when you serve these at your next barbecue feast.

Serves 4

1 pound White Lily Flour

2 tablespoons granulated sugar

1 teaspoon kosher salt

11 tablespoons unsalted butter, cut into ⅜ x ⅜ inch squares.

1½ cups buttermilk

1. Preheat the oven to 350°F. Grease a cookie sheet.

2. Sift together the flour, sugar, and salt in a mixing bowl.

3. Add 8 tablespoons (1 stick) of the butter, cold and cubed, and very briefly work it into the flour with your hands. Each piece of butter should just be coated with flour. Add the buttermilk.

4. Mix *very gently* by hand until dough forms. You should still be able to see that some of the flour is not incorporated. That's a good sign!

5. Lightly flour a cool work surface. Gently roll out the dough to about 1½ inches thick.

6. Use a 3-inch-diameter round biscuit cutter to cut biscuits out of the dough. Reform and reroll the extra dough to the correct thickness, cutting more biscuits out of the leftover dough. (Refrigerate between batches.)

7. Place the biscuits on the cookie sheet, spaced evenly, and bake for about 15 minutes or until golden brown. Remove and brush with 3 tablespoons of the melted butter. Serve warm with a little honey butter or our Virgil's Maple Butter (page 116).

Note: Dust biscuit cutter in a bit of flour in order to prevent sticking.

Pure and Simple Potato Salad

If summer had its own salad, it would be this one. The combination of basic spices, creamy mayonnaise, sturdy potatoes, and some crunchy veggies just seems to go perfectly with a bright sunny day and a filling meal eaten outdoors. The smooth blend of flavors in our version of this summer standard sets the stage for ribs, brisket, or even barbecued chicken. The creamy nature of this salad cuts right through the heavy tastes you'll find in most barbecue and gives your tongue a little something extra to think about and enjoy.

Serves 4–5

2 pounds large red potatoes

2 teaspoons kosher salt, divided

1 cup mayonnaise

½ teaspoon celery seed

2 teaspoons finely diced green bell pepper

2 teaspoons finely diced celery

3 tablespoons finely diced yellow onion

2 tablespoons Dijon mustard

⅛ teaspoon ground white pepper

4 tablespoons chopped bread-and-butter pickles

1½ tablespoons sliced scallions, green part only

3 hard-boiled eggs, chopped

1. Place the potatoes in a 2-quart saucepan, cover with cold water, and add 1 teaspoon of the salt. Bring to a boil. Cook until fork tender.

2. Drain the potatoes and spread on a sheet pan. Refrigerate until entirely cooled, preferably overnight.

3. Combine the rest of the ingredients in a large mixing bowl and blend thoroughly.

4. Dice the cold potatoes into medium cubes. Add them to the dressing, carefully fold together, and refrigerate for at least an hour before serving, so that the flavors blend.

Beer-Batter Onion Rings

There's a place in heaven for the person who dreamed up wrapping sweet yellow onions in a crunchy crust. Add beer to that crust and you have a super little side dish that works equally well with true hearty barbecue like spareribs, and lighter fare like a grilled burger. Heck, these are even a great addition to your next game-day spread. We whipped up a unique spice blend for our beer batter, one with lots of scintillating savory flavors. Don't be surprised if you find yourself eating them long after you should have moved on to the main course. Like we warn our customers, these are more than a little bit addictive.

Serves 4–6

Flour Mixture

2 pounds all-purpose flour

¾ cup granulated garlic

½ cup granulated onion

3 tablespoons kosher salt

Batter

6 extra-large eggs

⅔ cup all-purpose flour

2 tablespoons baking powder

2 teaspoons cayenne pepper

1 tablespoon kosher salt

1 teaspoon paprika

1½ teaspoons lemon pepper

1½ teaspoons garlic powder

½ teaspoon onion powder

¼ teaspoon dried basil

1½ cups ale beer

Onions

2 pounds large yellow onions, peeled and cut into ¾-inch slices

4 cups canola oil

1. Sift all the ingredients for the flour mixture together into a large bowl.

2. Blend the eggs for the batter in the bowl of a stand mixer with a paddle attachment on medium, or in a large mixing bowl if using a hand mixer.

3. Reduce the mixing speed to low and add all the batter dry ingredients. Beat until incorporated. Add the ale, and transfer the batter to a large shallow bowl or baking dish.

4. Set up a breading station with the flour mixture, the batter, and a clean sheet pan.

5. For each onion ring, dredge the onion in flour, then in the batter, then in the flour again. Place the twice-breaded onion ring on the sheet pan (making sure to keep ring separated), and repeat the process until you've breaded all the onion rings. Refrigerate the rings for 10 to 15 minutes or fry immediately.

6. Add the oil to a large and deep sauté pan or electric skillet, so it is one-third full, and heat it to 340°F.

7. Fry the rings in batches, being careful not to crowd the pan. Remove to a paper towel–lined plate and let cool for several minutes before serving, to prevent burns.

Suggested Serving: Serve with ranch dressing.

Pickled Beets

This is a Southern favorite, but folks outside of barbecuing circles don't seem to be too familiar with it. That's a darn shame, because there are few things in this world that can't be made better with a little pickling. Beets just seem to come to life when pickled, with a more complex flavor than dill pickles (another barbecue favorite). We just love the briny tartness, and the hint of sweetness that remains even after you've properly prepared these root veggies. You can munch as many as you like because these ruby-colored sides are chock full of antioxidants and other good things that will keep your heart strong and your blood pumping. Doesn't hurt that they pretty up any barbecue table spread!

Serves 6–8

2½ pounds medium beets, cleaned but not peeled

2 tablespoons kosher salt

1½ tablespoons pickling spice

12 whole cloves

1¼ cups red wine vinegar

¾ cup granulated sugar

½ medium red onion, sliced

1. Place the beets in a 4-quart (or larger) pot, cover with water, and add the salt. Bring to a boil.

2. Reduce to a simmer and cook for 35 to 45 minutes, or until the beets are fork tender.

3. Drain the beets and spread on a sheet pan. Refrigerate for 1 hour.

4. Wrap the pickling spices and cloves in a piece of cheesecloth, and tie closed to create a sachet.

5. In a small saucepan, combine the vinegar, sugar, onion, and sachet with 2 cups water. Boil for 15 minutes. Remove from heat and let cool.

6. Peel the beets and cut them into ½-inch cubes. Add them to the cooled marinade and refrigerate for 24 hours before serving.

Ceviche de Camarones

Ceviche comes to barbecue culture from the depths of South America, where it was originally developed as a way to "cook" and keep seafood without refrigeration or the hassle of building a fire. The idea is a simple one: citric acids from limes and lemons cure the rich seafood, keeping it from spoiling and creating a sparkling flavor medley in the process. Barbecue lovers on the coast of Florida and Louisiana were the first to add this dish to cookout menus, but it's spread far and wide now, and for good reason—it's a great way to wake up your tongue with a fresh blast of fruity, spicy seafood, clearing the way for just about any style of barbecue. We make ours with a healthy dose of tasty shrimp, which provides a much richer flavor than those made with white fish.

Serves 6–8

1½ pounds Jumbo shrimp, peeled and deveined

½ pound Jumbo lump crab

½ cup fresh lime juice (4 to 5 limes)

½ cup fresh lemon juice (4 lemons)

1½ cups tomato juice

¾ cup clam juice

¾ cup orange juice

1½ cups ketchup

½ large yellow onion, finely diced

1 medium cucumber, peeled, seeded, and finely diced

1 avocado, peeled, pitted, and finely diced

½ pound fresh Roma tomatoes, quartered, roasted, and diced

3 tablespoons chopped fresh cilantro

1 jalapeño pepper, seeded and finely diced

½ cup finely sliced scallions

1 teaspoon ground cumin

1½ teaspoons kosher salt

½ teaspoon chopped fresh garlic

1 teaspoon hot sauce

Salt and pepper to taste

Avocado slices, for garnish

1. Slice each shrimp diagonally, into four pieces. Combine in a small bowl with the lime and lemon juices and refrigerate for 2 hours.

2. Combine the remaining ingredients, except the lump crab and garnish, in a large mixing bowl. Add the marinated shrimp to the mixture. Refrigerate for 2 more hours.

3. Taste, season with more salt and pepper as necessary, and serve garnished with avocado slices, crab, and fresh tortilla chips.

5

Rubs, Marinades, and Sauces

Keeping meat tender and flavorful over a long cooking process has always been the challenge of true barbecuing. Fortunately, pitmasters long ago met that challenge in spades. Experienced barbecue cooks use rubs, marinades, and—to a lesser degree—sauces to add some bite that accents the food's own flavor, and to keep moisture inside the 'cue, where it belongs.

Rubs got their name from the way they're applied. These dry spice combinations are massaged right into whatever you're intending to barbecue. Some rubs add just a little bit of special spiciness, while others bring big-time flavor. They can create just a thin layer of moisture-sealing goodness on the outside of the food or, as with a rub on a brisket, can be a part of a thicker "bark." In the end, though, the goal is always to add a bit more flavor and keep the food good and moist.

Marinades are meant to soak the food for longer periods, allowing the flavor of the marinade to go deeper into the tissue of the meat. They, too, help keep moisture in.

Sauces are some of the most incorrectly used condiments in any barbecue pantry. Truth is, many barbecue purists consider sauces sacrilege. Cooks work hard to create great tasting 'cue and they tend to frown on someone sloshing a whole bunch of sauce over the top of their creations. At Virgil's, we have nothing against sauces.

Heck, we even make and sell our own. But you should taste your barbecue before you add a sauce, because you might be surprised how good the food is dry. If you add sauce during the cooking process, it's generally best to wait until the last few minutes of cooking time. Most barbecue sauces contain a good deal of sugar, which can burn over time and give your barbecue an unpleasant taste.

The coatings that follow are the ones we've had the most success with in our restaurants. These are time-tested recipes, but there's no law that says you can't play with them a little bit to put your own mark on your cooking. Most serious grill jockeys are always adjusting and trying out new rubs, marinades, sauces, and coatings, because you just never know when you might strike taste bud gold. If you do decide to experiment, however, start simple. Going complex right out of the gate can lead to flavor confusion and less-than-perfect barbecue.

The wonderful thing about most of these recipes is that they are quite adaptable. You'll find the coatings that follow are used in different recipes throughout this book, but you should also feel free to experiment by using them in casseroles, stews, and other dishes. The flavors are terrific no matter where they're used. All these recipes create generous amounts, so there should be enough to use on multiple cookouts or different grilled and barbecued foods.

Carolina Vinegar Sauce

Much like barbecue has its regions, different areas of the Carolinas fancy different formulas for their sauce. Barbecue fanatics in many parts of North and South Carolina consider a mustard-and-vinegar base to be the foundation of traditional Carolina sauce. We've put a bit of our own spin on this regional specialty, combining a sugar-and-ketchup base with vinegar for a special blend of tart and sweet.

Makes 1 quart

1½ cups apple cider vinegar

1½ cups ketchup

1¼ cups packed light brown sugar

2 teaspoons cracked black pepper

1 tablespoon kosher salt

2 teaspoons celery seed

1½ teaspoons red pepper flakes

1½ teaspoons chili powder

½ teaspoon cayenne pepper

½ teaspoon ground cinnamon

½ teaspoon ground nutmeg

Combine all the ingredients with 3 cups cold water in a 3-quart (or larger) saucepan. Whisk together and bring to a boil. Reduce to a simmer and cook until the sauce is reduced by a little more than half. Allow to cool and refrigerate prior to use.

★ Mopping Up ★

Some old-time pitmasters use what are known as "mops," sauces applied during cooking to keep the moisture and flavor locked into the meat. The name comes from the method of applying them. The old salts tending to the barbecue would dip an actual mop in a bucket of sauce and swab the meat.

Virgil's Dry Rub

Every pitmaster has his own special rub recipe and this is ours (well one of them, anyway). It combines a real nice base of sweetness cut through with some fire to keep things interesting. The great thing about this rub is that it lets the flavor of the food come through, accenting rather than overpowering. We find that it's an ideal rub for just about any food you might cook on a grill, and can even liven up pan-roasted dishes like pork loin.

Makes 5–5½ cups

2½ cups sweet paprika

1 cup granulated sugar

½ cup Texas-style chili powder

½ cup minced onion

½ cup granulated garlic

¼ cup dried parsley flakes

6 tablespoons kosher salt

Combine all of the ingredients in a medium bowl and whisk together until completely incorporated. Transfer to a covered bowl with a tight-fitting lid. Store in a cool, dry place.

Virgil's Creole Seasoning

True Louisiana Creole cooking is a mix of different styles, including French, Caribbean, and Spanish. As you might expect, spices play a big part in the cuisine, and that's why this rub features a festival of spices that makes for a little New Orleans Mardi Gras parade on your tongue.

Makes 4 cups

2 cups seasoning salt

½ cup paprika

½ cup granulated garlic

½ cup cracked black pepper

2 tablespoons granulated onion

1 tablespoon cayenne pepper

1 tablespoon dried oregano

1 tablespoon dried thyme

Thoroughly mix the ingredients together in a covered container. Cover and store in a cool dry place.

 Virgil's Kitchen Tip

With the healthy amount of dry rub our Creole Seasoning recipe creates, you're sure to have some extra left over. That's good, because it's well suited to much more than just traditional barbecue. This dry rub is a great way to add loads of flavor to meat and poultry that are already tender but that might be a little light on the taste buds, like filet mignon and boneless, skinless chicken breasts. Sprinkle a little rub on both sides, grill 'em up, and get ready for those flavor fireworks!

Virgil's Mild BBQ Sauce

We're trusting that you won't let this slip out—this is a recipe between you and us, and don't nobody else need to know. We spent a long time working on this formula, to create the perfect balance of spice and sweet, dark and light, and sharp and soft. We think it's just about perfect for topping any barbecue, from pulled pork sandwiches to grilled chicken. Whip up a batch and you be the judge.

Makes 1 quart

3½ cups ketchup

⅓ cup dark molasses

½ cup loosely packed light brown sugar

1 cup white vinegar

2½ tablespoons Worcestershire sauce

3½ tablespoons soy sauce

2 tablespoons yellow mustard

¼ teaspoon hot sauce

1 tablespoon granulated garlic

1 tablespoon granulated onion

1 tablespoon chili powder

1½ teaspoons dry mustard

1½ teaspoons ground coriander

1½ teaspoons ground cinnamon

1½ teaspoons ground cumin

1½ teaspoons cracked black pepper

1 teaspoon red pepper flakes

½ teaspoon ground nutmeg

⅛ teaspoon cayenne pepper

1 tablespoon liquid smoke

Combine all the ingredients with 2½ cups cold water in a 3-quart (or larger) saucepan. Whisk together and bring to a boil. Reduce to a simmer until the sauce is reduced by a little more than half. When the consistency is that of loose ketchup, transfer to a storage container. Allow to cool and refrigerate prior to use. The sauce will keep for months.

Mustard Vinaigrette

There ain't nothing so useful as an all-purpose salad dressing. This is one of the best, and it will appeal to just about any palate. It is definitely savory and flavorful without being too overwhelming. Don't limit it to salads, though, it's just as great on fish, grilled veggies, lean cuts of pork, and skinless chicken.

Makes 2 cups

6 tablespoons Dijon mustard

⅓ cup red wine vinegar

1 cup olive oil

1 tablespoon chopped shallots

1 tablespoon chopped garlic

1 tablespoon, plus 1 teaspoon chopped onion

⅛ teaspoon kosher salt

1. Combine the mustard and vinegar in a large mixing bowl. Gradually add the oil in a thin stream while continuously whisking, until thoroughly blended.

2. Add the remaining ingredients and blend.

Texas Chili Spice Mix

The heart and soul of this terrific spice mix is the guajillo chili—one of the best chili peppers to come from our neighbors to the South—and the smokiness of chipotle powder. This chili pepper is commonly used in tamale salsas and other condiments because it's not going to set your tongue on fire, but it brings a mess of fruity flavor anywhere it goes. This blend makes for one-of-a-kind chili, and don't be surprised if you like it so much you start adding it to other dishes, like vegetable stew.

Makes 1 cup

2 tablespoons guajillo chili powder

2 tablespoons chipotle powder

6 tablespoons ground cumin

4 tablespoons dry Mexican oregano

4 tablespoons sweet paprika

Combine all the ingredients in a medium mixing bowl. Transfer to a covered container and store in a cool, dry place.

Fabulous Fried Chicken Marinade

The secret to incredible fried chicken is to make sure the meat does not get dried out. This marinade is your guarantee against dried-out chicken and dull flavor. It's got some kick to it, but it fits right in with the crispy nature of good fried chicken, and it will leave you wondering how simply frying something can make it taste so darn good.

Makes 1 quart

1 cup buttermilk

1 cup hot sauce

3½ tablespoons Fried Chicken Spice Mix (page 166)

Combine all the ingredients with 2 cups cold water in a medium mixing bowl. Transfer to a covered container and refrigerate overnight to allow all of the flavors to blend.

Fried Chicken Spice Mix

We use this mix to zest up our fried chicken, but don't let the name fool you—it's great on all kinds of barbecued and grilled poultry. It's got a mother lode of flavors from sweet to salty and everything in between. We think you're going to love this one so much, you might just try a dab or two on fish.

Makes 2 cups, plus 2 tablespoons

6 tablespoons kosher salt

6 tablespoons sweet paprika

5 tablespoons onion powder

5 tablespoons garlic powder

3 tablespoons dry mustard

3 tablespoons cracked black pepper

1 tablespoon ground cumin

1 tablespoon dried thyme

1 tablespoon poultry seasoning

1 tablespoon dried oregano

1 tablespoon dried sage

1 tablespoon chili powder

Thoroughly blend all of the ingredients in a medium mixing bowl and transfer to a covered container. Keep in a cool dry place until needed.

Universal Flour

We call it a flour, but it's actually a super-tasty, super-crispy fried crust just waiting to happen. Adding cornmeal to the mix makes for an appealing crunch, and the spices are just enough of an accent to give some kick to whatever's being fried, without overpowering the main ingredient's flavors. We use this mix on all kinds of fried fish and our popular fried chicken, as well. Once you taste it, you'll be looking for new ways to incorporate this blend into your cooking. Just keep in mind that the amount of mix in this recipe is enough for a big meal; if you're having a smaller affair, you might want to cut everything in half.

Makes 3¼ cups

1 cup yellow cornmeal

2 cups all-purpose flour

1 tablespoon granulated garlic

1 tablespoon granulated onion

1 tablespoon kosher salt

1 teaspoon dry mustard

1 teaspoon dried oregano

1 teaspoon dried thyme

1 teaspoon cracked black pepper

¼ teaspoon cayenne pepper

Combine all of the ingredients in a medium bowl. Whisk together until incorporated. Transfer to a covered container. Store in a cool and dry place.

Fried Turkey Marinade

If you plan on frying up a turkey breast, much less a whole turkey, you have to take steps to make sure that bird stays juicy. This marinade is sure to lock in the moisture no matter how long it takes to fry up the food, and the spice blend is going to lend a front-of-tongue goodness to the final product. It's also a winner for roasted chicken!

Makes 2 cups plus extra

1 cup vegetable oil

¾ cup Worcestershire sauce

½ cup soy sauce

¼ cup paprika

¼ cup chili powder

¼ cup seasoning salt

¼ cup granulated garlic

2 tablespoons cayenne pepper

2 tablespoons ground cumin

6 dried bay leaves

Combine all of the ingredients in a medium mixing bowl and thoroughly blend together. Transfer to a covered container and refrigerate overnight to allow the flavors to meld.

Alabama White Barbecue Sauce

This sauce is particular to northern Alabama and has been made famous by Big Bob Gibson Bar-B-Q restaurant, where they use a white sauce on their chicken. Folks in Alabama know just how good this mayonnaise-based taste sensation is and they're as likely to use it on French fries or bread as they are to spread it all over any kind of barbecue. No matter what you use it on, though, it's a decadent accent that brings out the best in just about anything it touches.

Makes 3 cups

2 cups mayonnaise

1 tablespoon cracked black pepper

1 teaspoon kosher salt

3 tablespoons fresh lemon juice (about 1½ lemons)

1 tablespoon white vinegar

2 tablespoons granulated sugar

¼ teaspoon cayenne pepper

½ cup grilled, cooled, and minced yellow onion slices

Combine all of the ingredients in a medium mixing bowl. Transfer to a covered container and refrigerate overnight to allow the flavors to blend.

Mushroom Gravy

If you like mushrooms, you are sure as shooting going to love this sauce. It's got a nice base of wine and beef broth that makes for a rich complement to the mushrooms, all of which goes perfectly with just about any meat or fowl, but especially grilled food. You can even put it over grilled veggies for a treat that will leave your stomach and your tongue mighty satisfied.

Makes 4 cups

9 tablespoons unsalted butter, divided

½ cup all-purpose flour

4 cups beef broth

2 tablespoons chopped shallots

2 (6-ounce) packages crimini mushrooms, sliced thin

½ cup Cabernet Sauvignon

¼ teaspoon kosher salt

⅛ teaspoon cracked black pepper

1. Melt 6 tablespoons of the butter in a 2-quart saucepan over medium heat. Add the flour and mix to form a roux. Cook on low for 4-6 minutes, until a nutty brown color is reached.

2. Slowly whisk in the beef broth. Reduce to a simmer and cook for 15 minutes.

3. In a separate sauté pan, combine 1 tablespoon of the butter and the shallots. Sauté for 3 minutes. Add the mushrooms and cook for 5 minutes. Add the wine and whisk to dissolve the residue in the pan. Reduce the sauce until almost dry.

4. Add the sautéed mushroom mixture to the thickened broth and simmer for an additional 10 minutes. Add the salt and pepper and finish with the remaining 2 tablespoons of butter. Serve immediately.

6 ★

Beef

The story of beef barbecue begins with Texas. Texas has been cow country since long before it was a state, and now, of course, it's the Longhorn State. But the lure of barbecuing beef has spread far and wide since the early days; grilling and barbecuing beef cuts large and small has become a countrywide obsession.

Shouldn't be surprising. Barbecue began largely as way to cook inferior cuts of beef so that they would be tender and tasty. That's always been at the heart of cooking low and slow—it gives the fat in the meat time to completely "render" or melt into the meat

A colorful rub turns into the tastiest "bark" you could ever want on a brisket.

and tenderize it. This process can work magic on less-than-perfect cuts of beef, like a brisket.

But the other side of beef is that favorite weekend activity, grilling. Many's the man (and the woman) who finds heaven in the perfectly grilled steak. And, of course, what would the world of outdoor cooking and backyard picnics be without the good old hamburger, crisscrossed with char marks and dripping with juicy goodness?

Let's just face it: beef is pretty much the king of the grill.

The recipes that follow are the most popular beef dishes we serve in Virgil's. They represent the full range of barbecuing techniques and beef cuts. You'll find classic Texas brisket (page 173) that requires slow cooking for the better part of a day, and a tried-and-true T-bone (page 201) that takes less than a quarter of an hour to travel from refrigerator to plate. The variety is reflected in the many flavors these dishes represent. The one thing that they all share, though, is that they are plumb delicious and filling in a way no other protein can be. So fire up the cooker, smoker, or grill and get your steer on; it's time for a good old beef cookout!

Cow Close-ups

Barbecue, and especially beef barbecue, has been a staple in big-budget Westerns—and other movies as well—since Hopalong Cassidy took his first shot from the hip. An old-fashioned steer barbecue has played a walk-on part in big budget flicks that include *McLintock!* with John Wayne; *The Right Stuff*, with Sam Shepard; *Giant*, with James Dean; and, of course, Mel Brooks's *Blazing Saddles*, among many others. Even Hollywood can't resist the allure of barbecued cow.

True Texas Brisket

A brisket is a big cut of beef and just the thing for feeding a lot of hungry friends some real, honest-to-goodness quality barbecue. The cut is ringed with fat that makes it self-basting, and it's usually prepared, as in this recipe, with a flavorful dry rub. The rub ensures the signature "bark," a crusty layer that adds a distinctive texture and is just flat-out delicious. Follow the instructions here and use a nice fruit-wood for smoke, and you'll give your meat the definitive smoke ring that sets great brisket apart from the merely good. Just be careful when cutting the brisket—you must cut across the grain to serve the meat at its most tender.

Serves 12–14

2½ tablespoons kosher salt

2 tablespoons cracked black pepper

1 (11–15 pound) beef brisket, excess fat trimmed to within ½ inch all around

2 cups Virgil's Dry Rub (page 159)

1. Mix the salt and pepper and sprinkle evenly over the brisket. Follow with a coating of the dry rub, applied evenly all over. Enclose the brisket in a tightly covered container and refrigerate overnight.

2. Preheat the smoker or grill to 240°F, and load with a generous amount of apple wood (or substitute other fruitwood, as desired) mixed with oak or hickory. Place the brisket to the side of the heat source and cook for 13 to 15 hours, or until tender. The brisket is properly cooked when the meat thermometer reads 185°F, and the meat provides little resistance to the probe.

3. Remove the brisket and allow it to rest for 45 minutes. Cut into thin slices, slicing against the grain.

THE RIGHT BEER: When you serve up perfect brisket, you want to accompany it with beer that has plenty of body and richness, but that's not too "hoppy"—something like a pale ale, a brown, or an amber. The beer should let the brisket's heavy flavors play loud, while refreshing the palate after every sip. We serve Sierra Nevada Pale Ale, Brooklyn Brown Ale, Cisco Whale's Tale Pale Ale, Shipyard Old Thumper Extra Special Ale (English bitter), and Stone Smoked Porter with our brisket.

Virgil's Bacon Cheeseburger

There is just something soul-satisfying about a properly grilled burger with all the trimmings. It's an awfully simple thing to make, but that doesn't mean you shouldn't go ahead and make the best one in the world. We think we've done that by paying attention to all the little details in our recipe. We use just salt and pepper to season the meat, because a great hamburger lets the taste of the meat shine through. For the same reason, you shouldn't use lean chuck for your burgers, because the fat provides a lot of rich flavor and helps keep the burger moist. The other secret to a world-class beef patty is to not overwork it. Put it on a hot grill, flip once, and call it a day. We slide ours onto a sesame brioche bun that provides the perfect stage for all that meaty goodness.

Serves 1

½ teaspoon kosher salt

⅛ teaspoon cracked black pepper

8 ounces ground chuck

2 slices bacon, cooked crisp

1 slice cheddar cheese

1 sesame brioche bun

1 tablespoon unsalted butter

1 leaf Boston bib lettuce

1 thin slice red onion

1 slice ripe beefsteak tomato

4 kosher pickle chips

1. Mix the salt and pepper into the beef using your hands. Form a patty but don't overwork it.

2. Preheat the grill on high. Place the patty on the grill and cook to desired temp (160°F is recommended by the USDA, although medium-rare is 140°F to 150°F),

about 4 minutes each side. Only flip the burger once and whatever you do . . . *don't press the burger!*

3. While the burger is cooking, slice the bun and open it up. Generously butter each side and lightly grill to toast.

4. Add the cheese on top of the burger and let it melt. Remove the bun and burger, and assemble the burger from the bottom up: lettuce, tomato, onion, burger, sliced bacon, pickles, and the top of the bun.

THE RIGHT BEER: A classic burger like ours calls for an easy drinking lager that you can gulp down and that will quench your thirst. Nothing fancy, just a good, solid drinking beer. We wouldn't hesitate to serve Budweiser or Lone Star with our burgers, but we also like them with Coney Island Lager or Full Sail's Session Lager. For something really different and neat, try 21st Amendment Hell or High Watermelon Wheat Beer served in a can.

Virgil's Shopping Tip

Any burger you grill can only be as good as the meat you buy. Be careful when you're shopping and buy the freshest ground chuck possible. You can have a local butcher ground your chuck for a really delicious burger, but most people are going to have to select from the meat counter at the local supermarket. Do yourself a favor and check the date on the packages to buy the one that's been wrapped the most recently. Then check the fat content. You're looking for beef around 20 percent fat (remember that the fat accounts for most of the taste and moistness in a burger).

Chicken Fried Steak with Country Gravy

There's a special place in the Comfort Food Hall of Fame for this decadent dish. When you pound a piece of steak flat, you tenderize the heck out of it. Bread and fry that steak, and you have a slice of heaven on your plate. The only way to make that heaven better is to drown it in country gravy. We make our version of this Southern diner classic with some special flavors in the breading, and a dose of sage in the gravy that really brings it to life. Serve this with your favorite barbecue or as a weeknight happy times meal—either way, you're going to find out firsthand why the very heart of barbecue country, Lamesa, Texas, holds an annual festival dedicated to chicken fried steak.

Serves 6

Country Gravy

1 tablespoon canola oil

¾ pound bulk breakfast sausage

4 tablespoons unsalted butter

½ cup finely diced yellow onion

½ teaspoon finely chopped fresh sage

¾ teaspoon dried sage

½ teaspoon poultry seasoning

¼ teaspoon kosher salt

¼ teaspoon ground white pepper

4 tablespoons all-purpose flour

1 cup heavy cream

2 cups chicken stock

Chicken Fried Steak

1 (36-ounce) beef eye of round

2 teaspoons kosher salt

2 teaspoons cracked black pepper

3 cups lightly crushed plain potato chips

3 cups lightly crushed saltine crackers

3 cups corn flakes

1 cup Universal Flour (page 167)

4 extra-large eggs, beaten

3–4 cups canola oil

1. Make the gravy in a large saucepot with a heavy bottom. Combine the oil and sausage over medium heat and lightly brown the sausage. Break it up into quarter-sized pieces. Add the butter and onions and continue to cook until the onions are translucent.

2. Add the sages, poultry seasoning, salt, and pepper. Sprinkle in the flour and stir to form a roux. Cook for an additional 2 minutes. Add the cream and stir until thickened. Add the chicken stock and continue to lightly simmer for another 3 minutes, or until the mix has thickened into a gravy.

3. Slice the trimmed beef eye of round into six 6-ounce portions.

4. Cover a large cutting board with plastic wrap and lay out two of the steaks, 3 to 4 inches apart. Place another piece of plastic wrap on top and gently pound the steaks with a meat mallet until they are about 3/8 inch thick. Uncover the steaks, dust with some of the salt and pepper, and set aside. Repeat until all the steaks have been flattened.

5. In a medium mixing bowl, combine the potato chips, crackers, and cornflakes. (Be sure that the chips and crackers are crumbled to the size of the corn flakes to ensure uniform breading.)

6. Set up a breading station with the pounded-out beef steaks, a pan with the Universal Flour, a bowl with the eggs, and the bowl filled with the cornflake breading mix.

7. To bread the steaks, dip each steak into the flour and dust off any excess. Then dip it into the eggs, and press the steaks into the breading mix. Repeat with each steak, and stack the breaded steaks on a plate, separated with sheets of parchment paper.

8. Fill a large and deep sauté pan, or an electric skillet, one-third full of the oil. Heat the oil to 350°F.

9. Fry the steaks, one at a time, for 1½ to 2 minutes per side, or until golden brown. Place the fried steaks on a sheet pan covered with 3 to 4 layers of paper towels. Don't stack the steaks.

10. Serve the steaks warm, smothered in the gravy, with Perfect Buttermilk Biscuits (page 141) on the side.

THE RIGHT BEER: The filling richness of a chicken fried steak calls for a mild-flavored ale or pale ale, either of which will let the hearty gravy grab the starring role. We serve our Chicken Fried Steak with Sierra Nevada Pale Ale, Rogue Dead Guy Ale (pale ale), Anchor Steam Beer, or Cisco Whale's Tale Pale Ale.

Kansas City Burnt Ends Sandwich

One thing true barbecue pros never do is waste something if they can help it. Matter of fact, many barbecue operations started out as ways to make use of meat that wasn't sold during the day, and for lack of refrigeration would go bad if not cooked overnight. Barbecue folk just aren't the type of people who go in for throwing away anything that can be put to good use. Which brings us to this particular delicacy. Burnt ends are bits and pieces trimmed off the point ends of a brisket, and tell you what, they can be just as tasty as the original source. We stuff them in a sandwich that is chock full of other savory ingredients, including spicy, mouthwatering sausage and even our own crunchy onion rings. There's pretty much everything on this sandwich but the kitchen sink, and that's only because we didn't have one to spare.

Serves 1

2 ounces smoked andouille sausage, cut lengthwise

5 ounces burnt ends (cut from the brisket, page 173)

2 tablespoons unsalted butter

2 slices Texas Toast

2 tablespoons Horseradish Mayo (page 186)

2 tablespoons Virgil's Mild BBQ Sauce (or substitute your favorite mild barbecue sauce)

3 Beer-Batter Onion Rings (page 145)

1. Preheat the oven to 400°F.

2. Lay the sliced sausage on a small sheet pan along with the burnt ends and bake for 3 minutes.

3. Spread butter on one side of each slice of bread. Toast the bread, butter side down, in a medium-sized sauté pan over medium-low heat. When the bottom is lightly toasted, remove the bread and liberally spread the mayonnaise on each slice. Spread the warm burnt ends on one slice of the toast.

4. Lightly coat the meat with the barbecue sauce, and top with the onion rings. Layer the sausage on top. Cover with the other slice of toast.

5. Slice the sandwich in half and serve with dill pickles, Hickory Pit Baked Beans (page 112), and Grandma's Collard Greens (page 110).

Horseradish Mayo

2 cups mayonnaise

¾ cup sour cream

5 tablespoons horseradish, drained and any liquid squeezed out

Zest of 1 lemon

¾ teaspoon cracked black pepper

½ teaspoon kosher salt

In a small mixing bowl, fold all of the ingredients together. Refrigerate overnight in a covered container before serving or using.

THE RIGHT BEER: Burnt ends are traditionally paired with a rounded, full-bodied beer, something with strong fruity notes. We like to partner our Burnt Ends Sandwich with Captain Lawrence Brown Bird Ale, Shipyard Old Thumper Extra Special Ale (English bitter), or Captain Lawrence Liquid Gold (Belgian-style ale).

The Story of Texas Toast

All things are bigger in Texas. Don't take our word for it, just ask any Texan. That being the case, Texas barbecue shacks could not condone using regular old normal-size bread for barbecue sandwiches. Legend has it that the idea for Texas Toast came from The Pig Stand restaurant, which was a chain of barbecue joints back in the 1940s. A bakery delivered overly thick-cut bread that the cook discovered was perfect for capturing all the juiciness of a barbecue sandwich. It probably also appealed to the locals' need for big everything. Because barbecue cooks regularly buttered and toasted the thick-cut bread on the griddle, it came to be known as "Texas Toast." Which just goes to show you, even the story of plain old bread is bigger in Texas!

Smoked Brisket Hash

Those who know their stuff say that you haven't really ever had hash until you've had yourself some true brisket hash. We tend to agree. This recipe goes to show the versatility of a well-smoked brisket—it can improve just about anything it touches. It's also a wonderful way to make the best use of leftover brisket. This is a simple, filling pleasure, one that relies on turning the mix as it cooks so that the exposed outside edges of the brisket and potatoes become crispy. That makes for a satisfying crunch when you eat it; a sprinkling of cilantro adds a little sparkle to this heavy dish, and gives it a nice finish.

Serves 2

2 tablespoons corn oil

½ cup finely diced yellow onion

2 cups boiled, cooled, peeled, and diced red potatoes

½ teaspoon kosher salt

½ teaspoon cracked black pepper

½ pound True Texas Brisket (page 173), coarsely chopped

5 tablespoons Virgil's Mild BBQ Sauce (or substitute your favorite mild barbecue sauce)

2 tablespoons chopped fresh cilantro

1. Preheat the oil in a medium sauté pan. Add the onions and sauté until lightly browned.

2. Add the potatoes, salt, and pepper, and sauté until browned. Add the brisket and barbecue sauce and stir to combine.

3. Increase the heat slightly and cook until the bottom of the hash develops a crispy crust. Fold the hash over. Repeat this process.

4. Fold one more time and remove from the heat. Add the cilantro. Taste and adjust the seasonings as desired, and serve hot.

 **THE RIGHT BEER:** Any kind of hash—but especially brisket hash—calls for a sturdy, full-bodied beer. When you factor in the barbecue sauce in our version, the beers that work best are Brooklyn Brown Ale, Shipyard Old Thumper Extra Special Ale (English bitter), Dixie Blackened Voodoo Lager, or Stoudt's Scarlet Lady Ale E.S.B.

The Brisket Melt

This is the true barbecue fan's version of the classic patty melt. As sandwiches go, you won't find one that fills the belly and satisfies the soul better. We think rye bread must have been invented to be paired with brisket because the subtle flavor of the bread is a perfect background for the strong, rich flavors of the smoked meat. We use sharp cheddar because it can hold its own against any kind of barbecue. The rest of the ingredients are just as simple and delicious as the day is long. As with many barbecue dishes, there's just no need to complicate things when you create such a hearty appetite killer with the basics.

Serves 1

3 tablespoons unsalted butter, divided

½ medium yellow onion, thinly sliced

2 slices seeded rye bread

2 slices sharp cheddar cheese

7 ounces True Texas Brisket (page 173)

3 dill pickle slices

1. Combine half of the butter and the sliced onions in a sauté pan over medium heat. Sauté until the onions pick up some color, turning light brown. Set aside.

2. Use the remaining butter to coat one side of each bread slice. In a clean large sauté pan over medium-low heat, toast the bread, butter side down. Top each slice with a cheese slice and cover with the onions.

3. Top each slice with the brisket and leave in the pan until the bread is toasted on the underside of each piece, and the cheese is melted.

4. Fold the halves into a sandwich. Slice the sandwich in half and serve with pickles, Virgil's Simple Slaw (page 121), and Pure and Simple Potato Salad (page 143).

THE RIGHT BEER: Just as you would with brisket, you want to accompany this sandwich with beer that has plenty of body and richness, but that's not too "hoppy"—something like a pale ale, a brown, or an amber. The beer should let the brisket's heavy flavors play loud, while refreshing the palate after every sip. We serve Sierra Nevada Pale Ale, Brooklyn Brown Ale, Cisco Whale's Tale Pale Ale, Shipyard Old Thumper Extra Special Ale (English bitter), or Stone Smoked Porter with our melt.

Smoked Pastrami

If you love traditional deli pastrami, you're going to flip for smoked pastrami. Actually, traditional pastrami is technically smoked—at temperatures well below 100°F (known as "cold smoking"). The pastrami is also cured and steamed. We've put our own spin on this deli favorite to create a taste sensation that takes the original up a notch. Simple brining adds the characteristic salty flavor, but our blend of spices makes for a super-delicious marinade that intensely flavors the pastrami and ensures that it doesn't dry out during the long smoking process. One word of caution, though: be careful in the choice of wood that you use to smoke this pastrami; fruit-woods will tend to give the meat flavors that compete with the spice blend.

Serves 6–8

Brine

½ cup kosher salt

6 cloves garlic, smashed

2 tablespoons pickling spice

5 dried bay leaves

1 (9–11 pound) beef brisket

Marinade

3 tablespoons kosher salt

½ cup dark molasses

6 tablespoons chopped garlic

4 tablespoons chopped ginger

4 tablespoons granulated sugar

2 tablespoons ground coriander

2 tablespoons fennel seed

1 tablespoon cracked black pepper

1 tablespoon ground white pepper

1 tablespoon ground allspice

1 tablespoon ground cloves

1. In a stockpot with a heavy bottom, combine all of the brine ingredients with ½ gallon cold water, bring to a boil, and continue boiling for about 20 minutes.

2. Remove the brining liquid from the heat, set aside, and allow to cool to room temperature. Transfer to a large covered glass bowl, and refrigerate for at least 1 hour and up to overnight.

3. Trim the fat from the brisket, so that only ¼ inch remains all around. Submerge the brisket in the chilled brine for 24 hours. You can use a brining bag made especially for this purpose (available at most supermarkets) or a large covered container that will fit in the refrigerator. If there is no space in your refrigerator, you can use a cooler, but regularly add ice to keep the brisket chilled.

4. Combine the marinade ingredients in a small bowl. Remove the brisket from the brine and discard the brine. Pat the brisket dry, and coat evenly all over with the marinade.

5. Refrigerate the brisket in a covered container for 48 hours.

6. Preheat the smoker or grill to 250°F. Remove the brisket and allow it to come to room temperature, approximately 2 hours.

7. Smoke the brisket for 8 to 10 hours, or until fork tender. Remove from the smoker or grill and refrigerate overnight. Slice to desired thickness.

 **THE RIGHT BEER:** The heavy, rich nature of a smoked pastrami calls for a beer that is both lightly refreshing and features a bit of acidity and hops. Cut through the pastrami's heavy spices and richness with pale ales and IPAs. We like to serve it with Red Hook IPA, or Ballast Point Big Eye IPA.

Virgil's Smoking Tip

The biggest challenge you'll face with the smoked pastrami recipe is keeping a grill at the low temperature of 250°F over the duration necessary to smoke the brisket. A charcoal grill can usually be moderated to lower temperatures by keeping vents mostly closed once the coals are embers. Gas grills take more attention. Keep the burners as low as possible and bring the temperature up slowly when you start. If you find that the temperature won't stay down, you may have to create a false lid out of a tent of aluminum foil (the foil will conduct heat away from the cooking chamber much quicker than the lid of the grill will). You can also use a large disposable foil roasting pan placed on top. Weight it down and poke holes in it to further regulate the smoke and temperature. In any case, you should work with a quality thermometer and check it regularly throughout the cooking process. Never assume a grill—or even a smoker—is maintaining the desired temperature.

Smoked Corned Beef

You don't need the luck of the Irish to enjoy the best corned beef you ever tasted. The secret is revealed in this recipe, and it's in the smoking, which adds a little bang to the traditional rich savory flavor of corned beef (which is actually brined brisket). Smoking is a simple process, but it takes a long time, so this is a good weekend recipe. Plan on checking on the smoker or grill frequently, to ensure that the low temperature is kept steady. If you're looking to slice the smoked corned beef for sandwiches, put it in the refrigerator overnight—that makes it easier to slice it thinly.

Serves 8–10

1 (6–8 pound) corned beef brisket

6 tablespoons pickling spice

1. Trim the fat off the corned beef, leaving a ¼-inch layer all around.

2. Fill a stockpot three-quarters full of cold water and add the pickling spice and beef. Bring to a boil and reduce to a simmer. Cook for about 3 hours.

3. While the beef is boiling, preheat the smoker or grill to 250°F.

4. Remove the beef from the water and smoke it for 4 hours. Remove from the smoker and allow it to rest for at least 20 to 30 minutes. Serve with your favorite sides or traditional boiled cabbage.

Smoked Corned Beef Reuben

There's just something really satisfying about a properly made Reuben sandwich. It's a perfect blend of salty flavors with the slightest undertone of sweet, and meaty goodness balanced against a light cheese. (We use a special Swiss cheese that is extremely flavorful but doesn't have the sharp bite of some versions.) The rye bread is the classic shell used for this sandwich and we think it adds something to the taste of the meat, so try to use the best rye you can find. The sandwich itself is reason enough to smoke up a big Smoked Corn Beef (page 195).

Serves 1

3 tablespoons unsalted butter, divided

⅓ cup sauerkraut

2 slices seeded rye bread

3 tablespoons Virgil's Thousand Island Dressing (page 72)

7 ounces sliced Smoked Corned Beef (page 195)

2 slices Emmentaler cheese

1. Preheat the oven to 400°F.

2. In a medium sauté pan over medium heat, combine half of the butter and the sauerkraut. Sauté until most of the liquid evaporates and the sauerkraut is heated through. Set aside.

3. Brush one side of each bread slice with the remaining butter. Use a clean sauté pan over medium-low heat, and toast the bread, butter side down.

4. Spread the dressing on both slices, and pile the corned beef on one slice. Cover with sauerkraut and then top with the cheese.

5. Place the sauté pan in the oven for one minute, or until the cheese melts. Cover with the top slice, cut the sandwich in half, and serve.

THE RIGHT BEER: Just as with smoked pastrami, smoked corned beef really begs to be paired with a beer that is thirst-quenching, acidic, and hoppy. The best beers to go with the sauerkraut and Thousand Island Dressing in this recipe are IPAs, farmhouse ales, and pale ales. We suggest you try Goose Island Sofie (Belgian-style ale), Porkslap Pale Ale, or Lagunitas IPA.

Virgil's Grillin' Tip

There's a bit of art and science to getting a steak to just the right level of doneness. Because temperatures differ between grills and even with the same grill under different conditions, cooking time is an unreliable indicator of doneness. Instead, you'll want to use an instant read thermometer poked into the meat away from any contact with the bone. Listed in the table below are the temperatures at which you should remove the meat from the heat source. Allowing the meat to rest before serving is essential not only for saturation of flavors and juices, but also because it continues to cook to a modest degree. We've provided the temperatures used by our own pitmasters and experts, and the temps that the USDA recommends. (The USDA always recommends higher temperatures to ensure food safety, as well as requiring a 3-minute rest period after cooking.)

	Recommended by Virgil's	Recommended by the USDA
Rare	125	145
Medium rare	130	145
Medium	140	145
Medium well	155	160
Well done	160	160

Some grillers swear by more folksy tests, like squeezing different parts of your hand and comparing that to the feel of poking the meat. But at Virgil's, we feel testing the temperature is the best way to determine doneness. After you grill up a few steaks, you'll develop a good sense for when they're done on your grill, using whatever fuel you use. Practice makes perfect.

Classic Grilled T-bone

When you have a hankering for steak, there's just no substitute. And if you're going to grill one up, you might as well use the very best cut (in our humble opinion). The T-bone steak includes sections of loin and tenderloin that guarantees you're going to enjoy the tastiest beef to be found. It doesn't take much to grill this cut to perfection. We recommend you buy Angus beef and then use some very basic seasonings that let the rich flavor of the meat come through. Make sure you don't overhandle the steak, grill it quick, and you'll find it's easy to satisfy your hankering in a big way.

Serves 1

1 (20-ounce) Certified Angus Beef T-bone steak

2 tablespoons olive oil, divided

1 teaspoon garlic powder

1½ teaspoons kosher salt

1½ teaspoons cracked black pepper

1. Season the steak by rubbing it all over with half the olive oil and sprinkling with the spices. Let it sit for at least 10 minutes before grilling.

2. Heat the grill over medium-high heat. Grill the steak to the right temperature for your preferred doneness (see Virgil's Grillin' Tip on page 199). Flip the steak no more than twice, and whatever you do . . . don't press the steak!

3. Once the steak reaches the desired temp (level of doneness), remove it and allow it to rest for 2 minutes.

4. Cut the filet and the strip portions off the bone and slice each against the grain.

5. Place the bone on a plate and arrange the slices back on their respective sides of the bone. Lightly sprinkle with remaining olive oil and serve.

 **THE RIGHT BEER:** A good steak calls for a nice, full-flavored beer like a porter, stout, amber, or rye. We like to serve our T-bones with Laughing Dog Rocketdog Rye I.P.A., Stone Smoked Porter, Left Hand Milk Stout, or Abita Amber.

Texas Chili with Chipotle Cream

There's chili, then there's true Texas chili. We think it's the difference between jumping and flying, frankly. We don't go in for none of that ground beef in our chili; we use real, honest-to-goodness skirt steak for a meaty blend that just can't be beat. We also pack our recipe full of spices and other ingredients that give the final dish a ton of rich, smoky flavor and a stout, hearty body. As if that weren't enough, we top our chili with drop-dead delicious chipotle cream. It ups the ante on the smoky, pepper-driven flavor of the chili and is about a thousand times better than plopping some lifeless sour cream on top of our wonderful creation. This is terrific for big cookouts with lots of hungry folks to feed, or on cold winter nights when the whole family needs some warming up with filling and wholesome comfort food.

Serves 4–6

Chipotle Cream

10½ ounces goat cheese

2 tablespoons pureed chipotle in adobo sauce

1 cup plus 2 tablespoons heavy whipping cream

Juice of ½ lemon

Juice of 2 limes

Zest of ½ lime

½ teaspoon kosher salt

Chili

2 tablespoons Texas Chili Spice Mix (page 162)

¼ cup canola oil

2 pounds skirt steak

2 teaspoons kosher salt

⅓ pound sliced bacon, diced

4 cups finely diced yellow onions

2 cups finely diced green peppers

½ cup chopped garlic

1 (28-ounce) can crushed tomatoes, drained

2 tablespoons dark brown sugar

2 tablespoons dried Mexican oregano

2 tablespoons Texas-style chili powder (use 3 to 4 tablespoons for a thicker chili)

3 tomatillos, rinsed and diced

3 tablespoons corn masa flour (recommended: Masaca)

2 tablespoons pureed chipotle in adobo sauce

5 cups beef broth

2 (16-ounce) cans black beans

½ bunch cilantro, coarsely chopped, divided

1 (13-ounce) bag tortilla corn chips, crushed

1. Combine all the ingredients for the chipotle cream—except for the zest—in a food processor. Process until evenly incorporated.

2. Remove to a medium bowl and fold in the zest. Refrigerate for at least 2 hours before serving.

3. Mix the Texas Chili Spice Mix with the oil to make a paste. Dust the skirt steak with salt, then baste with the paste.

4. Marinate for 1 hour and then grill over high heat to medium rare. Set aside and allow to rest.

5. In a large, heavy-bottom pot, render the diced bacon until it is crispy. Add the onions, green peppers, and garlic, and sauté until slightly brown.

6. Add the tomatoes, brown sugar, oregano, chili powder, tomatillos, flour, and chipotles. Heat for 3 minutes, or until the mixture begins to thicken.

7. Add the beef broth, bring to a boil, and reduce to a simmer. Simmer uncovered for one hour.

8. Cut the steak against the grain into small cubes. Add the steak and beans to the chili, and simmer for an additional 20 minutes.

9. Add most of the chopped cilantro and serve over crushed tortilla chips with a dollop of chipotle cream and a sprinkling of fresh cilantro on top.

 **THE RIGHT BEER:** Chili is beer food, and the best beer to drink with our chili is one with a full, rounded flavor and a very clean finish. We prefer to serve our chili with pale ales, ambers, or ryes, such as Cisco Whale's Tale Pale Ale or Stoudt's Scarlet Lady Ale E.S.B.

Brisket Philly Cheese Steak

You got to be careful when you're messing with a classic, but we feel we've only made the traditional cheese steak better, and a lot of our visitors from Philadelphia seem to agree. Our version is the very heart of simplicity and makes great use of any extra brisket you might have lying around after a big cookout. The rest of the sandwich is just what you'd find in about three aisles of the local grocery store, but the sum of the parts is much greater than any single ingredient. For a lot of folks, this is the sandwich to end all sandwiches—a perfect marriage of cheesy appeal with meaty flavor and just enough rich onions to make the whole thing dance on your tongue.

Serves 1

½ cup diced yellow onions

1 tablespoon unsalted butter

10 ounces sliced brisket

3 slices American cheese

1 small French baguette, sliced lengthwise

1. In a medium pan over medium-high heat, sauté the onions in the butter until slightly browned. Chop the brisket up into coarse pieces and add it to the onions. Cook the mixture until it's hot.

2. Add the slices of cheese to the top of the mix in the pan. Give them a minute to melt and then remove the mixture with a spatula, and place on one slice of the bread.

3. Cover the sandwich with the remaining slice, and serve it up hot with a bunch of our Beer-Batter Onion Rings (page 145).

7 ★

Pork

Pork stands shoulder to shoulder with beef as a time-honored barbecue favorite. The great state of Texas may be all about the steer, but in the Carolinas, Tennessee, and beyond, the pig is favored. And to many barbecue fans, barbecued ribs are the dish that most screams "true barbecue."

Of course, there's much, much more to the pig than the ribs. Barbecued pork comes in many styles: pulled, chopped, pulled and chopped, different styles of ribs, tenderloin, Boston butt (the shoulder), ham (the leg), and more. Sweeter and often more tender than cuts of beef, pork is perfectly suited to the low-and-slow cooking method of true barbecue. It also is naturally well suited to sauces and rubs, and is generally easy to cook. All in all, this delicious white meat basically bridges the gap between chicken and beef in the barbecue world.

Pork is also incredibly versatile and makes for many different barbecue experiences. Few people will ever forget the first time they dove into a big pile of ribs and came away up to their elbows in sticky, gooey mess and the memories of delightfully sweet and smoky flavors haunting their tongue. Compare that to the old-time experience of standing in a meat market savoring the spiced tastiness of smoked sausage cut into thick discs and served plain on a square of butcher paper, with only a couple of pickles and crackers to keep it company. Such are the many faces of pork—a well-smoked loin and grilled pork chops can seem like they come from two different animals entirely. The point is, if you're considering pork for your next cookout, you're sure to find something for just about any taste or preference.

You'll find that diversity represented in the recipes that follow. We've included a little bit of everything where pork's concerned, from ribs to loin and back again. So get yourself some moist towelettes, fire up the grill or smoker, and start experiencing the tasty pleasure of pork.

 Virgil's Cooking Tips

All pigs have ribs, but not all pig ribs are the same when it comes to barbecuing. Barbecue pros generally talk about three categories of pork ribs: spare, baby back, and St. Louis. Baby backs are cut from the top of the rib cage, from where the pork loin stops and the spare rib begins next to the spine. They are taken from smaller hogs and are generally more curved, shorter, and meatier than spareribs (sometimes, because of their size, they may seem to have less meat than a sparerib but actually have a higher meat-to-bone ratio). Spareribs are cut from near the end of the rib cage, on the belly side. They begin where the baby backs end, and go all the way down. Spareribs with the sternum and rib tips removed are called St. Louis cut ribs and are the most popular style. The cut creates a rectangle and, because the ribs are more likely to contain some belly fat, both spare and St. Louis ribs are generally more tender and richer than baby backs. Beginning barbecuers are usually going to have an easier time with St. Louis cut ribs, and most butchers will gladly cut and trim the ribs at your request.

Memphis-Style Spareribs

There are two things people in Memphis never take lightly—their blues and their ribs. The blues are served up with plenty of soul, and the ribs are barbecued and served up dry. That means that any sauce is served on the side; the ribs are seasoned only with a dry rub that creates an incredibly flavorful crust. Properly smoked, these ribs have a telltale pink smoke ring and the meat is tender as the day is long. Do yourself a favor and trim the ribs (or have your butcher trim them) St. Louis style, so you wind up with two racks of ribs free of excess gristle and fat. Then just cook them with your favorite blend of spices, using a little hickory for smoke, and a bit of reverence for the fine folks in Tennessee who first came up with this heavenly dish.

Serves 4–6

2 (3¾–4½ pound) racks of spareribs

3 tablespoons kosher salt

2 tablespoons cracked black pepper

1½ cups Virgil's Dry Rub (page 159)

1. Prepare the racks of spareribs by peeling off the membrane that covers one side of the ribs. Trim away any loose fat. Cut away the breastbone using a boning knife, so that all the ribs are the same length. (If you prefer to have your butcher prepare the racks, ask him for a St. Louis cut.)

2. Sprinkle the ribs with the salt and pepper, followed by a coating of Virgil's Dry Rub. The spices should be spread evenly on both sides of the ribs.

3. Preheat the smoker or grill to 260°F, and add hickory—or your preferred wood—to the smoke chamber, or chips to the coals or burners.

4. Smoke the ribs for 3½ to 4 hours. They are done when the meat between the bones gives just slightly when pinched. Another way to determine if the ribs are

cooked is to pick up a rack with tongs and bounce it slightly. The outside surface between ribs will crack easily if the ribs are done.

5. Remove the ribs and allow them to cool for 10 to 15 minutes. Cut the individual ribs and serve.

 **THE RIGHT BEER:** Cut the rich, dense flavors of barbecued pork with a crisp, light-bodied beer, such as a lager or pale ale. We serve our Memphis spareribs with Rogue Dead Guy Ale (pale ale), Anchor Steam Beer, Magic Hat #9, or Dale's Pale Ale in cans.

Baby Back Ribs

If you ever ordered up a plate of baby backs in a restaurant like Virgil's, you know firsthand how delicious, tender, and meaty the ribs can be when smoked up right. Well, now you can work that same magic at home with this incredibly simple recipe. The way we make them, the meat pretty much just wants to jump off the bone and into your mouth, where it melts right on the tongue. The secret is giving the ribs enough time in the smoke so that the meat gets saturated with it and becomes as tender as tender can be. Be careful, though—one plate of these rich wonders, and they might become an every-night habit!

Serves 4

4 (2 pounds or less) baby back rib racks

6 tablespoons kosher salt

2 teaspoons cracked black pepper

1. Preheat the smoker or grill to 250°F.

2. Thoroughly season the rib rack with salt and pepper. Be sure to cover both sides. Place in the center of the grill or smoker, away from any direct heat source.

3. Smoke the ribs for approximately 3 to 4 hours, or until tender (the meat should begin to pull away from the bones). Remove and let rest for 10 minutes.

4. Cut the ribs between the bones, and serve with Virgil's Apricot BBQ Sauce (page 55) and Virgil's Habañero Key Lime Hot Sauce (available online or in our restaurants— or substitute your own favorite habañero hot sauce).

 **THE RIGHT BEER:** Although they have slightly different flavor profiles, we go with much the same beers for our baby backs as with our spareribs: Rogue Dead Guy Ale (pale ale), Anchor Steam Beer, Magic Hat #9, or Dale's Pale Ale in cans.

Boston Butt, the Virgil's Way

In case you were wondering (or a little concerned), the name comes from the barrels that this cut of pork were packed in for transport prior to the revolutionary war—barrels known as "butts." It's an unfortunate name for an awfully delicious cut of pork, but don't let it get to you: this is the shoulder of the pig and it's naturally less tender than the ham and certainly less than the loin. But a good long smoking levels out those differences and makes Boston butt a sought-after delicacy. We pull our meat off the bone to create "pulled pork," which is a bite-sized way of presenting the meat. And, as if the scintillatingly smoky meat wasn't enough of a draw, we mix up the pulled pork with a tantalizing combination of our spice-thick dry rub and tangy vinegar sauce.

Serves 6–8

1 (9–11 pound) bone-in pork shoulder (butt)

2 tablespoons kosher salt

2 tablespoons cracked black pepper

1½ cups Virgil's Dry Rub (page 159), divided

1 cup Carolina Vinegar Sauce (page 157)

1. Trim the excess fat off the pork, leaving about ½ inch all around. Thoroughly season with salt and pepper and then coat with about 1 cup of the dry rub. Be sure to cover both sides. Place the pork in a covered container and refrigerate for 24 hours.

2. Preheat the smoker or grill to 250°F.

3. Place the pork butt in the center of the smoker or grill, away from any direct heat source. Smoke for 10 to 12 hours, or until fork tender. Remove and let rest for 30 minutes.

4. Pull the meat off the pork butt and separate it. Remove the bone and all of the connective tissues and discard.

5. Liberally mix the meat with the vinegar sauce and the remaining dry rub, and serve.

THE RIGHT BEER: You can go with something lighter and sparkling to emphasize the flavors in this dish. We recommend ales, lagers, and golden ales. We serve our pulled pork with Rogue Dead Guy Ale (pale ale), Full Sail's Session Lager, Lone Star Beer (lager), or Captain Lawrence Liquid Gold (Belgian-style ale).

Perfectly Smoked Pork Loin

The pork loin is one of the most flavorful parts of a pig and can be prepared in many different ways. One of the best things you can do is to give it a long bath in a rich blend of spices, and then roast it until the meat just about falls off your fork. Our blend of spices is kind of a magic blend, if we do say so ourselves. It manages to hold its own with savory flavors that complement the rich taste of the loin, without making the meat taste like something else. A little bit of citrus brightens up the whole dish and adds some high notes to an otherwise spicy flavor. We suggest that you thoroughly cool the cooked loin in the refrigerator overnight and then slice it very thin before serving.

Serves 6–8

1 (4-pound) pork loin (center cut, if from a larger piece)

15 cloves garlic

1 tablespoon kosher salt

1 teaspoon ground cumin

1 teaspoon dried Mexican oregano

½ teaspoon ground black pepper

2 teaspoons cayenne pepper

¼ cup orange juice

Juice of 2 lemons

2 tablespoons sherry

2 tablespoons olive oil

½ pound yellow onions, coarsely diced

1. Score the pork loin with ½-inch-long and ½-inch-deep cuts on the surface of the meat. Slice each garlic clove in half lengthwise. Insert a piece of garlic in each cut on the loin.

2. Combine the remaining ingredients in a food processor and pulse to blend. Coat the loin with the mixture and refrigerate in a covered container, along with any extra marinade, for 24 hours (flip the loin halfway through the process).

3. Preheat the grill to 375°F.

4. Add a foil packet of hickory chips on the burners or coals. Place the loin on a sheet of aluminum foil or in an aluminum baking pan and roast in the grill for 20 minutes. Reduce the heat to 325°F and roast for an additional 45 minutes, until the internal temperature reaches 150°F.

5. Remove and let rest for at least 15 minutes before serving.

 **THE RIGHT BEER:** Like many types of pork, barbecued pork loin is best paired with light ales and lagers. At Virgil's, we like to sit our pork loin down next to a bottle of Rogue Dead Guy Ale (pale ale) or Anchor Steam Beer.

Virgil's Finger-Licking Rib Sandwich

Lots of people have tried to make a boneless rib sandwich to rival what they serve in the small barbecue shacks you can only find along two-lane roads in the wilds of the Southern states. But they haven't been there, like we have. And they haven't spent quality time savoring every bite of one of those sandwiches, and talked over the merits of putting rib meat on bread with the very barbecue scholars who do it so well. And that, ladies and gentlemen, is why ours is simply the best you're going to find (or, in this case, make). You may never eat another type of sandwich again. That's just how good it is.

Serves 1

½ rack baby back rib meat (about 8 ounces)

½ cup Virgil's Mild BBQ Sauce (or substitute your favorite mild barbecue sauce)

1 (6-inch) sourdough sub roll

1 tablespoon unsalted butter

½ cup Virgil's Simple Slaw (page 121)

1 medium pickled green tomato, sliced very thin

2 tablespoons mayonnaise

1. Heat up the rib meat and sauce in a small pot, over medium heat.

2. Slice the roll and open it up. Butter each side and lightly grill to toast, butter side down. Spread the slaw on the inside of the bottom half.

3. Add the rib meat and sauce. Top with the tomato and mayonnaise. Serve with your side of choice (we recommend fries or mac and cheese).

 **THE RIGHT BEER:** This sandwich begs for a clean, simple beer, such as a lager or pale ale. The Virgil's staff likes to serve our rib sandwich with Rogue Dead Guy Ale (pale ale), Anchor Steam Beer, Magic Hat #9, or Dale's Pale Ale in cans.

Slow-Smoked Ham

If a well-cooked ham doesn't bring back memories of a lazy summer Sunday afternoon spent enjoying the sound of the screen door slamming and the smell coming out of mama's kitchen, well, then you should have grown up in the South. Hams are taken mighty seriously in barbecue land, because the meat is so darn flavorful to begin with. We try real hard not to mess with that flavor, only make it better. And the way we do it is to smoke the ham a bit to give it some authentic barbecue flair, and then coat it in an incredible glaze that does the meat justice. (Just a word to the wise: let your ham sit out for about 2 hours prior to smoking; a ham that goes in at room temperature is more likely to cook evenly.) We've had folks ask us to sell them gallons of our Bourbon Creole Mustard Glaze, but we tell them the only place you'll find it is on our ham. Well, and now in your kitchen.

Serves 6–8

> 1 (12 to 14-pound) cured bone-in ham
> 1½ cups Bourbon Creole Mustard Glaze (page 228), divided

1. Trim the fat off the ham, leaving a ¼-inch layer all around. Use a sharp knife to score the surface of the ham into a diamond pattern.

2. Preheat a smoker or your grill to 250°F.

3. Smoke the ham for 1½ hours. Remove and liberally baste with about 1 cup of the glaze. Cook for about 1 hour more, or until the ham's internal temperature reaches 145°F. Periodically check the smoker or grill temperature throughout the cooking process.

4. Remove the ham, coat with the rest of the glaze, and allow to cool for several minutes prior to slicing.

Bourbon Creole Mustard Glaze

2 tablespoons finely diced yellow onions

2 teaspoons corn oil

3 cloves garlic, roasted

5 dried apricots, finely diced

3 tablespoons Creole mustard

1 tablespoon soy sauce

1 cup dark brown sugar

½ cup real maple syrup

1 cup fresh-squeezed orange juice

2 tablespoons bourbon

⅛ teaspoon cayenne pepper

Juice of 1 lemon

1. In a small pot over medium heat, combine the onion and oil. Sauté until the onions begin to pick up some color. Add the roasted garlic and diced apricots and sauté for 1 minute more.

2. Add the rest of the ingredients, except for the lemon juice. Reduce to medium-low heat and cook the mixture until it becomes syrupy, 15–20 minutes.

3. Add the lemon juice and immediately remove from the heat. Place in a serving bowl and cool slightly prior to serving or using.

THE RIGHT BEER: Smoked ham can stand up to a beer with a fuller body and a complex character, such as wheat beer, pale ale, or brown ale. We often pair this delicious pork with Captain Lawrence Brown Bird Ale, Breckenridge Agave Wheat, or even a hard cider.

★ 8

Poultry

Poultry is the blank canvas of barbecue. Chicken, turkey, and even game birds all have a lighter flavor and a more naturally tender texture than beef or pork. That means poultry of all kinds are perfect for picking up and amplifying the rich flavors of a rub, marinade, or sauce, not to mention woodsmoke. And whether you're grilling or barbecuing, most poultry is going to cook a whole lot quicker than a beef brisket or pork tenderloin (we're not counting that whole turkey you're planning on smoking for Thanksgiving!).

The tradition of poultry in barbecue centers on the chicken. Farmyard cluckers are a favorite at cookouts because they can be prepared in so many different ways that work perfectly with other barbecue and traditional side dishes alike. Why, just in this chapter alone we've included recipes for serving it up fried, barbecued and pulled, and jerked. Consider these starting points. You can take the ball and run with it by adding in your own spices, trying out your own sauces, and generally experimenting to find the hit for your household. Chicken is an especially good choice for the novice outdoor cook because it's an easy meat to get right, and you're not gambling quite as much time and money as you would by bringing home a full-sized cut of cow.

And, even though we like to think of barbecue as more of a soul-satisfying culinary treat than a health food, there's no getting past the fact that poultry is a lighter, healthier alternative to heavily marbled red meat. Doing the healthy thing is the same reason we look for the least processed birds we can find to serve our customers. These days we're fans of hormone- and antibiotic-free birds, and free-range are tastiest in our opinion.

No matter what poultry you settle on for your next cookout, the trick is to always keep the moisture in while making sure the bird is properly cooked all the way through. We use lots of ways to keep our birds tender and juicy, and you'll find those techniques in the recipes that follow. But you should check out the cooking temperature chart on page 200 to make sure that you're playing it safe. Once you have a good idea of the bird you want to cook and how hot it should be, fire up your grill or smoker and get to painting flavors on that canvas.

Classic Pulled Chicken

Pulled chicken is the Swiss Army knife of barbecue. It can be used in more ways than you can shake a stick at. The tender meat is used as a bed for Mexican mole sauces, can be served up on salad greens covered with a little ranch dressing, and is ideal in stews and soups. It even makes for one bodaciously good sandwich; we put ours on a soft sesame roll topped simply with slices of sweet yellow onion and dill pickles. You don't need anything more than that. Pulled chicken is traditionally mixed up with a simple barbecue sauce. We use a combination of sauces to create an incredibly tasty balance of tart and sweet. This is melt-in-your-mouth goodness that most people find pretty addictive. Because of that, and because this style of chicken can be used in so many other dishes—or if you have lots of mouths to feed—you might want to consider doubling the recipe. This pulled chicken makes one of the best leftover meals ever.

Serves 4–6

4½ pounds chicken thighs, bone in, skin on

½ cup kosher salt, divided

2½ tablespoons cracked black pepper

2 cups Carolina Vinegar Sauce (page 157)

1 cup Virgil's Mild BBQ Sauce (or substitute your favorite mild barbecue sauce)

1. Preheat the smoker or grill to 250°F.

2. Thoroughly season the chicken with the salt and pepper. Cover all sides. Place in the center of the grill or smoker, away from direct heat.

3. Smoke for about 3 hours, until the internal temperature is 165°F and the meat begins to fall off the bone. Remove and let rest.

4. When the chicken is cool enough to handle, pull the meat off the bone, separating out the skin, cartilage, and bones. Discard everything but the meat.

5. In a large mixing bowl, liberally mix the meat with the sauces. Serve immediately.

 **THE RIGHT BEER:** The flavors of pulled chicken really pop out when eaten with a cleaner, little bit lighter bottle of brew. At Virgil's, we recommend ales, lagers, and golden ales. We serve our pulled pork with Rogue Dead Guy Ale (pale ale), Full Sail's Session Lager, Lone Star Beer (lager), or Captain Lawrence Liquid Gold (Belgian-style ale).

Kansas City Fried Chicken

We like to please as many folks as possible when serving up the crowds at Virgil's restaurant, and that means keeping a diversity of dishes on the table. Fried chicken is just a natural partner to grilled standards like a good hamburger and cookout sides like potato salad. But it's also an incredible comfort meal all on its own. The secret behind our super-good Kansas City Fried Chicken is proper pan frying. You have to use the right oil—something a bit neutral like safflower or canola. The smoking point for flavorful oils like olive or avocado is just too darn low, so stay away from them for frying purposes. You also need to keep the temperature consistent, and that means checking with a thermometer and not crowding the pan. Make sure you drain the chicken well on some paper towels and give it a little rest so that nobody gets burned biting into it, and you'll wind up with a championship meal that would make any KC barbecue pitmaster proud.

Serves 4–6

½ cup buttermilk

½ cup hot sauce

5½ tablespoons Fried Chicken Spice Mix (page 166), divided

2 tablespoons kosher salt

2 (4-pound) whole roaster chickens, cut into 10 pieces each

5 cups all-purpose flour

2½ cups canola oil

1. In a large mixing bowl, thoroughly blend the buttermilk, hot sauce, 2 tablespoons of the Fried Chicken Spice Mix, salt, and 1 cup cold water.

2. Press the chicken pieces into the marinade. Place in a covered container (ensuring that the chicken is covered with marinade), and refrigerate for 24 hours.

3. Thoroughly combine the flour with 3½ tablespoons of the Fried Chicken Spice Mix in a medium bowl.

4. In a large and deep pan, or an electric skillet, add enough canola oil to fill the pan one-third full. Heat the oil to 350°F.

5. Set the marinated chicken next to the bowl of flour, close to the skillet. Remove a piece of chicken from the marinade, allow any excess to drain, then dredge in the flour mix. Shake off the excess flour and slide into the skillet.

6. Fry the chicken for 4 to 5 minutes on each side, or until the internal temperature reaches 165°F. Fry the chicken in batches, being careful not to crowd the skillet and maintain the right temperature.

7. Remove the fried chicken to a sheet pan covered with three or four layers of paper towels. When all the chicken has been fried and dried on the paper towels, allow to cool slightly before serving.

THE RIGHT BEER: Virgil's fried chicken is best complemented with mild beers that can cut through the hearty batter coating, such as pale ales and lagers. We like to serve this house specialty with Shiner Bock, Corona Extra, or Cisco Whale's Tale Pale Ale.

Smoked Turkey Breast

Barbecuing a whole turkey can be a downright overwhelming challenge, not to mention simply impossible, depending on the capacity of your grill. But you can have plenty of that turkey goodness and make things a little easier on yourself by smoking a turkey breast. Providing abundant tender and juicy meat, the breast is easier to handle and every bit as delicious. The secret lies in keeping the meat moist with a marinade. The moisture not only keeps the meat from drying out, it helps saturate the breast with the flavors from the marinade. This recipe makes good use of a marinade with a nice pickled flavor, but don't you be shy about experimenting a little with the marinade ingredients to find just the right blend of spices for your taste buds.

Serves 8–10

½ cup Virgil's Dry Rub (page 159)

2 tablespoons kosher salt

¼ cup granulated garlic

¼ cup hot sauce

2 tablespoons pickling spice

1 (14–16 pound) bone-in, skin-on turkey breast

¼ cup Virgil's Creole Seasoning (page 160)

1 tablespoon cracked black pepper

1. Combine the first six ingredients with 1 gallon cold water in a large stockpot and bring to a boil. Boil for 20 minutes, remove from the heat, and let cool to room temperature.

2. Transfer to a covered container and refrigerate for several hours.

3. Place the turkey breast in a large resealable plastic bag and add the cold marinade. Seal the bag and place upright in the refrigerator, ensuring the entire turkey breast is covered with marinade. Refrigerate for 24 hours.

4. Preheat the smoker or grill to 275°F. Use apple wood or hickory for the smoke.

5. Remove the turkey breast from the bag, drain, and pat dry with a paper towel. Dust with the Creole Seasoning and pepper, and place in the center of the smoker or grill, away from direct heat.

6. Smoke for 3½ to 4½ hours, or until the temperature inside the breast reaches 165°F. Remove the turkey and allow it to rest for 20 minutes before cutting and serving.

THE RIGHT BEER: Any kind of barbecued bird is really a canvas for the marinade, rub, mop, smoke, or sauce flavors. The underlying taste is understated, which is why we recommend beers with medium body and modest hops. Golden ales, pale ales, and ambers all work well with this turkey. We serve Victory Golden Monkey, Magic Hat #9, Goose Island Honker's Ale, or Abita Amber with our barbecued turkey.

Jerk Chicken

We have the island paradise of Jamaica to thank for "jerk" cooking, which is really just another style of barbecue. This particular recipe—like all good jerk recipes—centers around the noble habañero pepper. It adds a bit of heat, but not so much spice that you'll be looking for a way to put out a fire on your tongue. Our unique blend of spices is complemented by a healthy dose of dark rum, which adds a bit of rich sweetness. And because this version of barbecue is a little off the beaten track, we thought we'd throw in a side dish to match. So you'll find a recipe for totally unique Jerk Potato Salad on page 242 as well.

Serves 4–6

1 tablespoon dried thyme

3 tablespoons molasses

3 teaspoons kosher salt

2 teaspoons cracked black pepper

2 to 3 fresh habañero peppers, roasted, seeded, and finely chopped

½ cup white vinegar

1 cup diced yellow onions

2 cups chopped scallions, greens only

2 tablespoons olive oil

4 teaspoons ground allspice

4 teaspoons ground cinnamon

4 teaspoons ground nutmeg

1½ tablespoons chopped fresh ginger

Juice of 4 limes

Juice of 2 oranges

2 tablespoons soy sauce

2 tablespoons dark rum

2 (4-pound) whole roaster chickens

1. In a food processor, pulse all the ingredients except for the chicken, until just consistent. The mixture should still be slightly coarse.

2. Reserve 2 tablespoons of the marinade and set aside for the Jerk Potato Salad.

3. Put the chicken in a resealable container and cover with the marinade. Toss to ensure the chicken is evenly coated. Refrigerate for 12 hours.

4. Turn the chicken in the marinade, and refrigerate for an additional 12 hours.

5. Preheat the grill to about 300°F.

6. Arrange the chicken on roasting racks on the grill away from the heat source. (If your grill doesn't have clearance to cook the entire chicken, quarter them and grill on the grates.) Brush with the marinade before closing the lid. Smoke the chicken for about 90 minutes, or until the internal temperature is 165°F.

7. Remove the chicken from the grill and let rest for 5 minutes. Cut the chicken into quarters and serve.

Jerk Potato Salad

2 pounds red potatoes

1½ tablespoons kosher salt, divided

1½ cups mayonnaise

½ tablespoon fresh thyme leaves

½ tablespoon dry mustard

¼ teaspoon ground turmeric

2 hard-boiled eggs, coarsely chopped

½ cup coarsely chopped dill pickles

½ cup finely diced celery

¾ cup finely diced yellow onions

2 tablespoons Jerk Marinade reserved from making Jerk Chicken.

4 slices smoked bacon, cooked crisp and chopped or crumbled

1. In a medium saucepan, combine the potatoes, half the salt, and enough cold water to cover. Bring to a boil over high heat and cook until fork tender.

2. Remove the potatoes to a sheet pan and refrigerate overnight.

3. In a large mixing bowl, blend the remaining ingredients. Dice the potatoes into large cubes and add to the dressing. Fold to thoroughly coat, cover, and refrigerate for 1 hour before serving.

THE RIGHT BEER: A little bit of fruitiness cuts right through the jerk spices and provides a lot of refreshment between bites. That's why the Jerk Chicken at Virgil's is paired with fruit beers and wheat beers. We suggest Magic Hat Circus Boy (*hefeweizen*).

It's easy to roast peppers like the habañeros in the Jerk Chicken recipe, and the process brings out the best in the pepper's flavor. You can use roasted peppers in everything from salads and soups to sprinkled on top of your favorite barbecue. To roast habañeros, preheat the oven to 200°F. Cut each pepper in half and seed it. Toss the halves in a combination of olive oil, salt, and freshly ground pepper until they are well coated. Then roast in a baking dish for 1 hour, or until the peppers are shriveled.

Whether you're roasting hot peppers like habañeros, or bell peppers like these red peppers, char the skins to make them easy to remove.

Chicken, Crawfish, and Sausage Gumbo

We figure if you're going to have a gumbo-making party, chicken should be first on the invite list. Gumbo is about as Louisiana as you can get, and classic gumbo is rich with the seafood and spices common to bayou country. Experts say there's even a little voodoo magic in a well-made gumbo. Heck, we might agree; a bowl of our gumbo can transform the most stressed-out diner into one very happy, fulfilled customer. Although traditional gumbos use all kinds of protein (they've been made with everything from owls to possums), we like to make chicken the star of ours because the white meat acts like a sponge in soaking up all those fine Cajun spices. This is a filling meal all by itself, or served by the cup it's just about the best starter you could want for hearty barbecue like brisket.

Serves 4–6

2 pounds (4–6) bone-in, skin-on chicken thighs

4 teaspoons kosher salt, divided

2 teaspoons cracked black pepper

1 stick unsalted butter

8 ounces andouille sausage, finely diced

4 ounces Tasso ham, finely diced

2 cups diced yellow onions

1 cup finely diced celery

2 tablespoons chopped garlic

3 dried bay leaves

1 tablespoon gumbo filé powder

¾ teaspoon cayenne pepper

1 teaspoon chopped fresh oregano

1 teaspoon fresh thyme leaves

¾ cup all-purpose flour

1 quart (4 cups) clam juice

1½ quarts (6 cups) chicken stock

1 cup sliced okra

1 cup finely diced green bell pepper

1 cup finely diced red bell pepper

1 pound crawfish tail meat (substitute 16/20 shrimp if you can't find crawfish tails)

1. Preheat the oven to 350°F.

2. Season the chicken with 2 teaspoons of the kosher salt and the cracked pepper. Bake in a roasting pan for about 45 minutes, or until the chicken reaches 165°F.

3. Remove the chicken and allow it to cool slightly. Pull the meat from the bones, and separate it from the skin. Set aside the meat and discard the rest.

4. In a low and wide 6-quart (or larger) stockpot over medium-high heat, add the butter and sauté the sausage and ham with the onions, celery, and garlic. Cook for about 4 minutes.

5. Add the bay leaves, gumbo filé, cayenne, oregano, thyme, and the rest of the salt. Cook until the mixture begins to pick up some color.

6. Add the flour and stir in to form a roux. Continue to cook until the mixture turns a fairly dark brown.

7. Add the clam juice and stock, and whisk out the lumps. Add the okra and bell peppers, bring to a boil, then reduce to a simmer (the mixture should begin to thicken). Simmer for about 20 minutes.

8. When the texture becomes stewlike, add the pulled chicken and crawfish (include any liquid from thawed crawfish). Bring to a boil and then remove from the heat.

9. Taste and season with more salt, pepper, or cayenne, as desired. Remove the bay leaves. Serve with cooked long grain rice.

 **THE RIGHT BEER:** When it comes to gumbo, the best beer holds its own against all the filling richness and complex spiciness. Think brown beer, rye beer, or ESB (extra special bitter). At Virgil's, we recommend Laughing Dog Rocketdog Rye I.P.A. or Stoudt's Scarlet Lady Ale E.S.B. with the gumbo.

Barbecued Halves and Quarters

Each piece of this bird is going to have a rich, deep smoked flavor that we accent with a healthy dose of our subtly sweet Virgil's Mild BBQ Sauce. It's a combination fit for a king, but you're royalty enough to dive right in. Just bring a goodly amount of napkins, because sticky fingers are all part of the fun. Or go ahead and lick 'em—we're not ones to judge!

Serves 4–6

2 (4-pound) roasting chickens

1 tablespoon kosher salt

1 teaspoon cracked black pepper

1 cup Virgil's Dry Rub (page 159)

2 cups Virgil's Mild BBQ Sauce (or substitute your favorite mild barbecue sauce)

1. Preheat the grill or smoker to 250°F.

2. Thoroughly season the chicken with salt and pepper, and then coat with Virgil's Dry Rub. Be sure to cover all sides.

3. Place in the center of the grill or smoker, out of the way of direct heat. Cook for 3 to 3½ hours, or until the chicken is heated to 165°F.

4. Remove from the heat and let rest until cool. When ready to serve, quarter each chicken, place on the grill over medium heat, and generously baste with the barbecue sauce. Serve when the sauce thickens to a glaze.

 **THE RIGHT BEER:** A straightforward lager or pale ale, something with a clean finish, works perfectly with barbecued halves and quarters. You can turn to the tried-and-true Budweiser, Lone Star Beer (lager), Rogue Dead Guy Ale (pale ale), or Corona Extra.

9

Seafood

Seafood may be just one word, but it describes a whole ocean of potentially delicious barbecue and grilled favorites. If we're being honest here, there's a whole lot more grilling going on with seafood than true barbecuing. It's just the nature of the beast that waterborne creatures are smaller and quicker to cook. Of course, that doesn't make them any less tasty. In fact, seafood can be a great way to switch up your barbecuing routine—especially if you're the type to get in a rut by cooking one or two dishes again and again. A little diversity does a body good. And diversity goes a fair piece to describing the textures and the flavors available with different seafood. Why, fish alone can be firm or flaky, meaty or light, dark or as white as a sheet of paper. One thing they all share, though: they are plumb delicious when grilled properly. Add in a little smokiness here and some special spiciness there, and you're sure to have yourself a big winner on the table at the end of the day.

We give a nod to all the different types of seafood with the recipes in this chapter. We've included classics that can be made much quicker than most other grilled or barbecued dishes, so they're great for weeknights or whenever you're in a rush to get good food on the table. You'll also find recipes that can be whipped up inside the house, so they work even when it's too cold out to crank up the grill or smoker. Some of what you'll find here is adaptable to other meats. For instance, use our Blackening Spice Mix on page 264 to flavor pork chops and create a whole new twist on that white meat. Whatever the case, dive into the recipes that follow and discover all the treasures the fruit of sea offers the smart pitmaster.

Friday Night Fried Catfish with Tartar Sauce

You can't get much more "down South" than fried catfish. Outdoor cooks from the banks of the bayou to the lakes of East Texas know just how delicious this whiskered fish can be—especially when you fry it up to perfection. The crispy coating seals in moisture and creates a simple crust that lets the subtle flavor of the catfish shine through. Accent this delectable dish with our own special tartar sauce. You're going to love this particular condiment, and don't be surprised if you get a hankering to drop it on top of your favorite burger or even dip fries in it! Make a nice little meal by pairing up your catfish with a couple classic partners, Crispy Hush Puppies (page 121) and Grandma's Collard Greens (page 110), for an incredible spread that speaks with a strong Southern accent. Your taste buds will think they died and went to heaven.

Serves 4

Virgil's Tartar Sauce

¾ cup mayonnaise

1 hard-boiled egg, chopped

2 tablespoons capers

1 tablespoon finely chopped shallots

2 tablespoons chopped fresh parsley

Juice of ½ lemon

1 tablespoon finely chopped scallions, greens only

1½ tablespoons finely chopped celery

½ teaspoon Tabasco sauce

Catfish

2½ cups canola oil

2 cups buttermilk

¼ cup hot sauce

1 tablespoon Fried Chicken Spice Mix (page 166)

½ teaspoon Virgil's Creole Seasoning (page 160)

2 cups Universal Flour (page 167)

4 (7–8 ounce) fresh catfish fillets

2 lemons, cut into halves or wedges

1. In a small mixing bowl, blend all the tartar sauce ingredients. Cover and refrigerate overnight.

2. In a large, deep saucepan, heat the canola oil to approximately 350°F.

3. In a small mixing bowl, combine the buttermilk, hot sauce, Fried Chicken Spice Mix, and Creole Seasoning. Set out the Universal Flour in a separate small bowl.

4. Place the catfish in the buttermilk mixture for 3 minutes. Remove and dust with the Universal Flour. Shake off the excess and gently slide into the hot oil.

5. Fry the fillets for about 3 to 4 minutes, or until golden brown on one side. Flip and fry for 3 more minutes, or until golden brown. (Fry the fillets in two batches of two fillets each. They will be much easier to maneuver.)

6. Remove the fried fillets to a large plate covered in paper towels. Blot with paper towels to dry.

7. Serve immediately with ¼ cup of tartar sauce and a lemon half for each fillet.

THE RIGHT BEER: Make the most of traditional fried catfish with a crisp, light-bodied beer that has a touch of acidity and citrus. Lagers, farmhouse ales, Belgian ales, pale ales, and a few wheat beers work well with catfish. We serve ours with Goose Island Sofie (Belgian-style ale), Lone Star Beer (lager), Brooklyn Lager, Samuel Adams Boston Lager, or Magic Hat Circus Boy (*hefeweizen*).

Barbecued Shrimp

Shrimp is naturally delicious to start with, but a little grilling makes this seafood something extra special. There's a tradition in the Deep South of cooking "barbecued" shrimp in a pan (the sauce adds a smoky flavor), but we believe that true grilling brings out the delicate, rich sweetness in the meat. Add a bit of the sauce we use and, well, it's just about as heavenly as a little bite of goodness can get. We swear by the garlic sauce we use on our shrimp because garlic is a natural partner to shrimp, but you can tailor the sauce to suit your own preferences.

Serves 4–6

Garlic Barbecue Sauce

6 tablespoons unsalted butter, divided

1 teaspoon chopped garlic

1 cup Virgil's Mild BBQ Sauce (or substitute your favorite mild barbecue sauce)

2 tablespoons Virgil's Dry Rub (page 159)

Shrimp

8 (6-inch) bamboo skewers

2 pounds fresh jumbo shrimp

½ cup olive oil

4 tablespoons Virgil's Dry Rub (page 159)

2 lemons, cut into wedges

1. In a small pot over medium-high heat, combine 1 tablespoon of butter and the garlic for the garlic sauce. Sauté the garlic for 1 minute, add the Virgil's Mild BBQ Sauce and Virgil's Dry Rub, and heat to a boil. Remove from the heat, whisk in the remaining butter, and set aside to use as needed.

2. Soak the skewers in water overnight.

3. Peel and devein the shrimp, leaving the tails on. Lay 4 shrimp out on a flat surface. Align them so that they are coiled with the tails on the same side, facing in the same direction.

4. Slide a skewer through the shrimp. Run another skewer through the shrimp, parallel to the first and about ½ inch apart. (This will prevent the shrimp from spinning on a skewer.) Repeat this process until all of the shrimp are skewered.

5. Brush one side of the shrimp on the skewers with olive oil, then dust with the dry rub. Flip the skewers over and repeat the process.

6. Place the seasoned skewered shrimp in a container, cover, and refrigerate overnight.

7. Preheat the grill to high heat.

8. Reduce to medium heat and position the skewers over direct heat. Grill for 2 minutes, then flip and grill for 1 to 2 minutes more.

9. Remove the skewers from the grill and brush each with 2 tablespoons of the garlic sauce. Serve with lemon wedges and Virgil's Simple Slaw (page 121).

THE RIGHT BEER: Because these shrimp include a healthy dose of garlic sauce, a beer with a nice fruity flavor and sturdy body will work best. We like to put our shrimp on the table with golden ales and wheat beers, like Long Trail Blackbeary Wheat, Magic Hat Circus Boy (*hefeweizen*), Ommegang Witte (wheat ale), Victory Golden Monkey, or Magic Hat #9.

Virgil's Food Tip

Not all shrimp are created equal. In most grocery stores, you're likely to find terms like large, jumbo, and colossal, but there's not a regulated standard on what these mean. Your eyes will usually tell you what's what in terms of size, but here's a little more information to help you out. These are official size designations and the way we order our shrimp (for instance, we usually use U-15 for our Barbecued Shrimp.) Smaller sizes are listed by the number of shrimp you can expect per pound. The larger sizes are listed by gauge, like shotgun bores: the lower the number, the bigger the shrimp.

Shrimp sizes

Size	Avg. No. of Shrimp/Pound
Small (51/60)	55
Medium (41/50)	45
Large (31/35)	33
Jumbo (21/25)	22
Colossal (U-15)	13
Extra colossal (U-10)	6

Shrimp Po' Boy

Po' boy sandwiches are one more thing we have to thank New Orleans for. These handy meals were originally filling lunches for the working class of the city, people who didn't have the money to pay for anything fancy or the time to sit down and eat. In fact, the term is just the New Orleans' accented version of "poor boy." The original sandwich was stuffed full of the local seafood, breaded, and clapped between two doughy slices of French bread. We pay homage to the history of the po' boy with our version that rocks some serious spice and includes our own formulation of tartar sauce. We've heard from folks who visit the Virgil's in Times Square from Louisiana that this breaded wonder tastes just like home. We think that should be endorsement enough to make your own today.

Serves 1

1½ cups canola oil

6 tablespoons buttermilk

4 teaspoons hot sauce

½ teaspoon Fried Chicken Spice Mix (page 166)

⅛ teaspoon Virgil's Creole Seasoning (page 160)

¾ cup Universal Flour (page 167)

5 ounces fresh rock shrimp

1 (10-inch) French bread hero roll

4 tablespoons Virgil's Tartar Sauce (page 253)

¾ cup shredded iceberg lettuce

½ medium tomato, cut into 4 slices

3 dill pickle slices

1. In a medium pan with high sides, heat the canola oil to 350°F.

2. In a small bowl, mix the buttermilk, hot sauce, Fried Chicken Spice Mix, and Creole Seasoning. Set out the Universal Flour in a separate small bowl.

3. Soak the shrimp in the buttermilk mixture for about 3 minutes. Remove and thoroughly dredge in the flour. Dust off the excess and slide the shrimp into the hot oil (work in batches to ensure the pan does not become overcrowded).

4. Fry for 2 minutes, or until golden brown. Remove from the oil and place on paper towels to blot dry.

5. Slice the roll lengthwise (but not quite all the way through). Spread the tartar sauce on both sides of the roll and place the shrimp on the bottom half. Top with the lettuce, tomatoes, pickles, and the top half of the roll. Cut and serve.

THE RIGHT BEER: The tangy tartar sauce means that this particular sandwich pairs well with clean, crisp beers that are easy drinking, like pale ales and lagers. We would recommend Kona Longboard Island Lager, Rogue Dead Guy Ale (pale ale), Corona Extra, and even Budweiser.

Grilled Red Snapper

Snapper is one of the most popular white fishes in the world, and for good reason. It has a wonderful, slightly nutty, sweet flavor that really comes out when the fish is grilled. And it's not just the flavor: this particular fish seems to match up like a champ with just about any seasoning you can think of, from super hot Asian blends to more subtle herb mixes—and especially the Creole spin we use. Even people who don't much like fish eat this right up when we serve it at Virgil's. We think it's especially good with the Creole Jambalaya Sauce on page 264, although you might want to try our own tasty Tartar Sauce (page 253).

Serves 4

4 (8-ounce) red snapper fillets

¼ cup olive oil

2 teaspoons Virgil's Creole Seasoning (page 160)

2 lemons, cut into wedges

1. Preheat the grill on high heat.

2. Brush the top of each snapper fillet with olive oil. Dust very lightly with the Creole Seasoning.

3. Place the fillets rub-side down on the grill. Grill for 2 to 3 minutes, then gently turn over. Grill for an additional 2 to 3 minutes, or until the fish is flaky.

4. Serve with the Creole Jambalaya Sauce (page 264) and fresh lemon wedges.

THE RIGHT BEER: There are a whole lot of different and powerful flavors in this dish, especially with the spicy jambalaya sauce. Our suggestion is a beer with substance and body, but one that isn't too overpowering—something like a farmhouse ale, pale ale, or golden ale. We'd go with Goose Island Sofie (Belgian-style ale), Captain Lawrence Liquid Gold (Belgian-style ale), or Victory Golden Monkey.

 Virgil's Cookin' Tip

When you're serving up fish, whether it's grilled, fried, or sautéed, you can always make it a little bit better with the right sauce. We make an extra-special version for our fish dishes, one that brings the best of the bayou to the table. Whip up one batch of this incredible sauce and we're sure you're going to have a hard time serving fish without it. But don't stop there—this can be the perfect covering for pasta of all types, and even works its magic on grilled pork.

Creole Jambalaya Sauce

2 tablespoons olive oil

2 ounces andouille sausage, finely diced

2 ounces Tasso ham, finely diced

1 cup finely diced yellow onions

½ cup finely diced celery

½ cup finely diced green bell pepper

½ cup finely diced red bell pepper

2 cloves garlic, chopped

2 tablespoons chopped scallions, greens only

2 dried bay leaves

1 teaspoon chopped fresh basil

1 teaspoon chopped fresh oregano

½ teaspoon chopped fresh thyme

½ teaspoon ground cumin

¼ teaspoon cayenne pepper

2 large plum tomatoes, finely diced

2 (8-ounce) jars clam juice

¾ cup chicken stock

¼ cup heavy cream

Salt and pepper to taste

1. In a 3½-quart (or larger) pot, combine the olive oil, sausage, and ham. Sauté until the meats brown, then add the onions, celery, peppers, and garlic and sauté for 3 minutes more.

2. Add the scallions, herbs, bay leaves, and spices, and stir to combine. Add the tomatoes, clam juice, and chicken stock, and bring to a boil.

3. Turn down to a simmer and reduce by half, until the mixture has a thick sauce consistency.

4. Add the cream and simmer for 2 minutes. Remove from the heat and discard the bay leaves. Taste and add salt and pepper, as desired, before serving.

Cajun Blackened Redfish

Blacken a spice mix and you bring it to life in a way no other cooking can. If that spice mix is the crust on light, flaky fish, well, you've got a spice party ready to make any tongue happy as can be. We use a balanced blend of spices in our blackened fish recipe, one that provides a lot of interest for the palate without burning your mouth. We think heat can be overused and spicy hotness sometimes sacrifices flavor. But with our redfish, you're going to enjoy flavor galore, and a tender, sweet, and moist flesh that may just leave you wanting to whip up this Cajun specialty every night.

Serves 4

Blackening Spice Mix

1 cup sweet paprika

2 tablespoons dried oregano

2 tablespoons dried thyme

2 tablespoons granulated onion

2 tablespoons granulated garlic

1¾ tablespoons cracked black pepper

1½ tablespoons kosher salt

1 tablespoon cayenne pepper

Redfish

½ cup olive oil

4 (10-ounce) redfish fillets

3 tablespoons canola oil

1 cup Virgil's Remoulade (page 40)

2 lemons, cut into wedges

1. In a small mixing bowl, thoroughly blend the blackening spice mix. Store in a covered container until needed.

2. In a small mixing bowl, combine the olive oil and 4 tablespoons of the blackening spice mix, to form a loose paste. Liberally brush the top of each of the fish fillets with the paste.

3. Preheat a large cast iron skillet over medium-high heat.

4. Add the canola oil and lay the seasoned fillets gently in the pan, spice side down. Sauté for 3 to 4 minutes and then gently turn over.

5. Sauté for 2 to 3 minutes more or until the flesh just begins to flake. Serve with the remoulade and lemon wedges.

 **THE RIGHT BEER:** When you have the kind of sharp spices you'll find in a blackened fish like this, you want a fruit-forward beer that can stand up to the Creole flavors. We suggest summer seasonal beers and lighter wheat beers, such as Magic Hat #9 or Long Trail Blackbeary Wheat.

Catfish Po' Boy

The people who love to eat catfish love it for the flavor, which is the same reason a lot of people aren't too fond of it. Just the same, when you fry catfish up—and especially when you park it between two slices of delicious French bread—that flavor becomes quite muted. Like other fish, catfish tends to adopt the flavors that surround it, and in this case, that means our unique coating that creates a distinctly Louisiana flavor, with just a little heat but a lot of savory complexity. Your tongue's going to take a while in figuring out all that's going on, but it will be mighty happy in the meantime. If you're still a little shy about the flavor of the fish, we suggest you look for farm raised, which has a much milder taste at a very reasonable price.

Serves 1

1½ cups canola oil

6 tablespoons buttermilk

4 teaspoons hot sauce

½ teaspoon Fried Chicken Spice Mix (page 166)

⅛ teaspoon Virgil's Creole Seasoning (page 160)

¾ cup Universal Flour (page 167)

1 (8-ounce) fresh catfish fillet

1 (10-inch) French bread hero roll

4 tablespoons Virgil's Tartar Sauce (page 253)

1 cup shredded iceberg lettuce

½ medium tomato, cut into 4 slices

3 dill pickle slices

1. In a medium pan with high sides, heat the canola oil to approximately 350°F.

2. In a small bowl, combine the buttermilk, hot sauce, Fried Chicken Spice Mix, and Creole Seasoning. Set out the Universal Flour in a separate small bowl.

3. Soak the fillet in the buttermilk mixture for 3 minutes. Remove and thoroughly coat in the flour. Dust off excess flour and gently slide the fillet into the hot oil.

4. Fry for 3 to 4 minutes or until the bottom is golden brown. Flip and fry until the other side is golden brown, about 3 more minutes.

5. Remove to a plate covered with paper towels. Blot to dry.

6. Slice the roll lengthwise, but not quite all the way through. Spread tartar sauce on both sides of the roll. Lay the fish fillet on the bottom half, covered by the lettuce, then topped with the tomatoes and pickles. Close the roll, cut, and serve.

THE RIGHT BEER: As with our fried catfish, we like to accompany this sandwich with a lighter beer that is slightly acidic. Try Goose Island Sofie (Belgian-style ale), Lone Star Beer (lager), Brooklyn Lager, Samuel Adams Boston Lager, or Magic Hat Circus Boy (*hefeweizen*).

Crawfish Étouffée

Étouffée is French for "smothered," and that's just what you do with this dish: smother innocent white rice with a spiced-up stew filled with rich shellfish. This Cajun favorite puts that wonderful local crawfish to work in a mix with a boatload of vegetables and traditional Louisiana hot flavors. Although this dish is traditionally served over white rice—and that's the way we do it—it actually works great on pasta and even mashed potatoes. If you have a hard time finding the crawfish . . . time to move down South. But, seriously, you can always substitute lobster or less expensive 16/20 shrimp.

Serves 4

8 tablespoons unsalted butter

1½ cups finely diced yellow onions

½ cup chopped scallions, greens only

1 cup finely diced celery

1 cup finely diced green bell pepper

4 cloves garlic, chopped

4 tablespoons all-purpose flour

3 dried bay leaves

1 teaspoon cayenne pepper

1 teaspoon dried thyme

1 teaspoon dried oregano

2 teaspoons kosher salt

½ teaspoon cracked black pepper

5 cups clam juice

2 pounds crawfish tail meat

Juice of 1 lemon

1 tablespoon Tabasco sauce

1. In a medium saucepot, combine half the butter and the onions, scallions, celery, bell pepper, and garlic. Sauté until the vegetables become translucent.

2. Add the flour and cook for about 5 minutes, or until the mixture forms into a roux, or thick sauce.

3. Add the bay leaves, cayenne, thyme, oregano, salt, and pepper. Whisk in the clam juice, bring to a boil, and then reduce to a simmer. Simmer for 20 minutes.

4. Add the crawfish (including any liquid from thawed crawfish). Return to a boil and add the remaining butter.

5. Remove from the heat, remove the bay leaves, and add the lemon juice and Tabasco, and more salt, as desired. Serve over cooked white long grain rice.

 **THE RIGHT BEER:** The classic étouffée is traditionally served with golden or brown ales. We like to dish ours up alongside Dixie Blackened Voodoo Lager, Brooklyn Brown Ale, or Shipyard Old Thumper Extra Special Ale (English bitter).

★ Virgil's Grillin' Tip ★

The only thing better than crawfish in a Cajun dish is *grilled* crawfish in a Cajun dish. If you're willing to fire up your grill, you can add something special to the étouffée recipe or any recipe that calls for this bayou delicacy. The best way to grill these critters is by blanching. Buy "True Select" crawfish and boil them in salted water for 30 seconds, then toss them in a bowl full of ice and water to stop the cooking. Cut along the inside of the crawfish and devein them, making sure to remove the sack behind the eyes. Then rinse well to clean the shellfish completely. Grill them in a grill basket, moving the crawfish around occasionally. Grill over medium heat for about 5 minutes, or until the shells turn bright red and the meat is white and opaque.

Jambalaya

If you want to start a brawl in Louisiana, just say that all jambalaya is the same. Folks in the Big Easy know there are two types of this meat-and-seafood stew—the Creole version, which includes tomatoes, and the Cajun version, which doesn't. We make ours in the Creole fashion and, like all jambalayas, it includes just about everything but the kitchen sink. The mix of meat and seafood makes this dish both hearty and rich. You won't need to serve much if anything alongside it, because it delivers all the flavors and punch necessary for a full meal . . . and then some. Just keep in mind that jambalaya is little like jazz and dancing, it never hurts to put your own spin on it. The dish is incredibly adaptable and can even be a way to use up the odds and ends in your refrigerator meat keeper.

Serves 4–6

Seasoning Mix

1 tablespoon dried parsley flakes

1¼ teaspoons cracked black pepper

2 teaspoons kosher salt

1¼ teaspoons sweet paprika

½ teaspoon dried basil

1½ teaspoons dried thyme

¾ teaspoon ground white pepper

1½ teaspoons onion powder

1½ teaspoons garlic powder

Jambalaya

2 pounds boneless, skin-on chicken thighs

12 (16/20) shrimp, peeled, deveined, tail on

6 tablespoons unsalted butter, divided

¼ cup olive oil, divided

5 ounces andouille sausage, finely diced

4 ounces Tasso ham, finely diced

2 cups finely diced yellow onions

1 cup finely diced celery

1½ cups finely diced green bell pepper

1 tablespoon chopped garlic

3 dried bay leaves

1¾ cups converted rice

2 cups finely diced fresh plum tomatoes

1 cup clam juice

2 cups chicken stock

Salt and pepper, to taste

1. In a small bowl, blend the seasoning mix together and set aside.

2. Cut each chicken thigh in half, and evenly dust the thighs with 1½ tablespoons of the seasoning mix. Dust the shrimp with about 1½ teaspoons of the mix.

3. In a low and wide 6-quart (or larger) stockpot, add 1 tablespoon of the butter and 1 tablespoon of the olive oil. Sauté the shrimp for about one minute per side. Remove the shrimp and set aside.

4. Repeat the process with the chicken, using the remaining oil. Remove the chicken and set aside.

5. In the same pot, brown the sausage and ham. Add the remaining butter, onions, celery, bell pepper, garlic, and bay leaves and cook for 4 minutes.

6. Add the rice, stirring to coat it with the mixture. Sauté for 2 minutes. Add the tomatoes and cook for 3 minutes more.

7. Add the clam juice, chicken stock, and chicken thighs. Bring to a boil, and then reduce to a simmer. Cook for 30 minutes, and then check the rice for tenderness and ensure the chicken is cooked through.

8. Fold in the shrimp and cook for another 3 minutes. Remove the bay leaves, taste, add salt and pepper, as desired, and serve.

THE RIGHT BEER: Jambalaya, like étouffée, calls for a nice, solid brown beer, rye beer, or ESB (extra special bitter). At Virgil's, we serve it up with Laughing Dog Rocketdog Rye I.P.A. or Stoudt's Scarlet Lady Ale E.S.B..

10

Sweets

You may not think of desserts when you think of barbecue, but we suggest you think again. Yes, the main course takes center stage (especially when some good soul spent the better part of a day working hard over hot coals or burners), but meal-ending sweets have been a part of traditional cookouts since the very first Southern Sunday Church Social. There's just something refreshing about a little bit of sweet after a plate full of smoke and spice.

The secret to all of the recipes in this chapter is using simple, wholesome, and fresh ingredients. They're readily available at just about any grocery store. No need to search all over creation for some special item or another. No, these are just basic, filling recipes with a lot of history behind them. Each dessert contains the sort of homemade goodness that you might remember coming out of your mother's or grandmother's kitchen. Fact is, these are all tried-and-true favorites that have been served at cookouts for generations.

We've included traditional favorites like Classic Lemon Chess Pie (page 298), and more unconventional creations like our own Vanilla Porter Float (page 313). Pick the one that strikes your fancy and you're sure to have a hit for the final dish at your cookout.

A properly baked pie with a homemade crust (see page 282) is just about the perfect end to a summer barbecue.

Of course, these don't necessarily have to be served up on a picnic table to hit the spot. You'll find that some of these desserts, such as Red Velvet Cake (page 303), are ideal for special occasions like birthdays or holidays. Some, like our satisfyingly sweet and simple Pecan Pie (page 309), are already associated with holidays like Thanksgiving and Christmas.

But really, each of these is special in its own way and can make a memorable event out of any meal. As steeped as these dishes are in the history, love, and tradition of barbecue, they're plenty adaptable. The great thing about all the desserts that follow is that they can be just as wonderful served after a weekday stovetop meal or as your contribution to any old potluck. Today, tomorrow, or Sunday afternoon, truth be told, there's really no bad time for a Virgil's dessert.

Sweet Potato Pecan Pie

This is a couple of traditional Thanksgiving favorites combined into one impressive and unique dessert. Sweet potato pie has a much longer pedigree than pumpkin pie, because this sugary tuber has been baked into tarts as far back as the Middle Ages. But barbecue culture has put its own stamp on this dessert, incorporating a spice blend that gives the dish a Southern flavor. We decided to add in pecans, because the nut's flavor perfectly complements the richness of the sweet potato and provides a little crunch underneath all that creamy goodness. What sets our version apart from the rest is the layers that make for a mix of flavors in what is a fairly simple and basic pie. No matter how full your cookout guests might be, we guarantee they'll find room for a nice big slice of this pie—and maybe two!

Serves 4–6

Filling

3 pounds sweet potatoes

¼ cup light brown sugar

2 tablespoons granulated sugar

1 extra-large egg, lightly beaten

1 tablespoon heavy cream

1 tablespoon unsalted butter

1 tablespoon pure vanilla extract

¼ teaspoon kosher salt

½ teaspoon ground cinnamon

¼ teaspoon allspice

¼ teaspoon ground mace (or substitute a pinch of freshly ground nutmeg)

1 (10-inch) deep dish pie shell (or the make the Perfect Pie Dough shell, page 282)

Syrup

1 cup pecan pieces

¾ cup granulated sugar

¾ cup dark corn syrup

2 extra-large eggs

1½ tablespoons unsalted butter

2 teaspoons pure vanilla extract

Pinch of cinnamon

Pinch of kosher salt

1. Preheat the oven to 350°F.

2. Bake the sweet potatoes for one hour, or until very tender. Remove and discard the peels and combine the potatoes with the rest of the filling ingredients in the bowl of a stand mixer (or use a large mixing bowl with an electric hand mixer). Blend on medium until smooth. Set aside.

3. Toast the pecan pieces for the syrup in the oven for 3 to 5 minutes. Remove and let cool, leaving the oven on.

4. Mix the other syrup ingredients, blending with a paddle attachment on low for 1 minute.

5. Spread the sweet potato mixture on the bottom of the pie shell. Cover with the toasted pecans, and slowly pour the syrup on top. Bake for 40 to 45 minutes, or until the center is firm and does not jiggle.

6. Remove and let cool on the counter. Once cool, refrigerate overnight prior to serving.

The Perfect Pie Dough

There is nothing quite like a homemade pie to satisfy the soul as well as the stomach. Here at Virgil's, we make the crust, because although store-bought shells are all well and fine, a homemade pie crust is really the heart of a homemade pie and something awfully wonderful in its own right. This recipe is simple and produces a satisfyingly flaky crust.

Makes 3 shells

4 sticks unsalted butter, cold

1½ pounds all-purpose flour

2 tablespoons granulated sugar

¼ teaspoon kosher salt

1 cup whole milk

1. Dice the cold butter into small cubes.

2. Combine the flour, sugar, butter, and salt in a large mixing bowl (use a stand mixer, or an electric hand mixer). Mix on low with a paddle or dough hook until the ingredients are just incorporated.

3. Add the milk and blend just enough so that the dough collects into one piece. Remove the dough from the mixer and divide into three equal pieces.

4. Wrap and refrigerate or freeze until needed. When ready to use, remove the dough, allow it to warm, and roll it out on a floured surface to a little thinner than ¼ inch thick.

5. Line a pie pan with the dough and trim and crimp the edges.

6. Depending on the recipe you're baking, you may want to "blind bake" the shell—bake it for 10 minutes at 350°F filled with pie weights or dried beans.

Mama's Peach and Blueberry Cobbler

Let's just take a minute to sing the praises of any dessert that features seasonal fresh fruit. Few treats can beat it, and fresh fruit is rarely better than when it's tucked into a syrupy, sticky, crunchy cobbler. (Of course, in a pinch you can make this cobbler with frozen fruit for those winter dinners!) Cobblers are a traditional treat that dates back to the early days of the South, and they were and are often baked right over an open fire. Our version features a filling just bursting with natural fruit flavor and bubbling right up through the topping. The crunchy topping is dressed in sugar to create a tongue-pleasing lid on the cobbler. The hearty nature of this dessert is what makes it such a perfect ending for a barbecued meal.

Serves 5

Filling

¼ cup orange juice

¾ cup, plus 2 tablespoons apple juice, divided

¾ cup pineapple juice

¾ cup granulated sugar

¼ teaspoon ground nutmeg

1 teaspoon pure vanilla extract

½ teaspoon ground cinnamon

1 tablespoon, plus 1 teaspoon cornstarch

2½ pounds fresh peaches, peeled and coarsely diced

1 cup fresh blueberries

Topping

¾ cup all-purpose flour

¼ cup granulated sugar

1 teaspoon baking powder

¼ teaspoon salt

6 tablespoons unsalted butter, cold and finely diced

2 tablespoons whole milk

3–4 tablespoons turbinado sugar

5 scoops vanilla ice cream (optional)

1. Combine the orange juice, ¼ cup of the apple juice, and the pineapple juice, sugar, nutmeg, vanilla, and cinnamon in a medium saucepan over medium-high heat. Bring to a boil and cook for about 5 minutes, or until the sauce is reduced by half.

2. Thoroughly mix the cornstarch with the remaining apple juice in a small bowl. Add to the sauce, bring to a boil, and remove from the heat.

3. Add the peaches to the sauce and cook over medium heat until they just barely begin to soften. Add the blueberries, remove from the heat, and pour the fruit mix into a 2-quart casserole dish or, for individual servings, separate small casserole dishes or ramekins.

4. Preheat the oven to 350°F.

5. In a small bowl, combine the first five ingredients for the topping and mix well.

6. Add the milk and mix well. Sprinkle the topping on top of the fruit, and dust the top of the cobbler with turbinado sugar.

7. Bake for 35 to 40 minutes, or until the top is golden brown. Remove and let cool for 3 minutes. Serve topped with a scoop of vanilla ice cream, if desired.

Perfect Peanut Butter Pie

Peanuts have a long pedigree in the South. Two Southern presidents, Jimmy Carter and Thomas Jefferson, grew this tasty legume on their farms, and the history of peanut butter itself can be traced back almost two centuries. But using this perfect food in a pie is just one more gift the South has given the world. And what a gift. The smooth texture of this treat has made it a favorite among cookout fans everywhere, and the graham cracker crust is just as popular. Cooks find this dessert easy to make and handy for a cookout because it can be made far in advance and refrigerated until that perfect moment when the table has been cleared of barbecue. It's just tasty enough to be the perfect finish to a barbecued meal, and just light enough to keep your guests from feeling too full.

Serves 4–6

Pie Crust

1⅓ cups graham cracker crumbs

4 tablespoons light brown sugar

½ teaspoon salt

¼ cup all-purpose flour

1 stick unsalted butter

Pastry Cream

1 cup whole milk

4 tablespoons granulated sugar

4 tablespoons all-purpose flour

2 large egg yolks

¼ teaspoon pure vanilla extract

Pinch of salt

Pie

1 cup heavy cream

3 cups creamy peanut butter

4 tablespoons light brown sugar

Topping

Chocolate shavings

Peanut Brittle (page 290)

1. Preheat the oven to 350°F.

2. Combine the graham cracker crumbs, sugar, salt, and flour for the crust in a medium mixing bowl. Melt the butter in a small saucepan and add to the dry mix, mixing until thoroughly incorporated.

3. Press the crust mixture into a pie pan, spreading it evenly across the bottom and up the sides. Press another pie pan down on top to firm the crust. Bake for 10 minutes, or until set. Set aside.

4. Add all the pastry cream ingredients to the top of a stainless steel double boiler over medium-high heat. When the water boils, whisk the ingredients continuously until they thicken to a pudding texture.

5. Remove from the heat and put the top of the double boiler in a large heat-proof bowl filled with ice. Occasionally fold the mixture over until completely cooled. Refrigerate overnight.

6. Whip the heavy cream for the pie until the beater forms a stiff peak, and then refrigerate.

7. Combine the peanut butter and brown sugar in a large mixing bowl and beat until the sugar is entirely incorporated. Fold in the pastry cream with a spatula until the mixture is completely blended.

8. Gently fold the whipped cream into the peanut butter mixture. Pour the mixture into the pie shell and shake back and forth to evenly distribute the filling. Refrigerate overnight.

9. Serve topped with chocolate shavings and Peanut Brittle.

★ A Fragile Treat ★

Brittles—hard toffee candy made with nuts—are popular around the world, with each country adding its own nuts. Peanut brittle has been wildly popular for well over a century in America, and rightly so. The candy is full of fun crunch and tantalizingly sweet caramel flavors, which is why we thought it would be the ultimate garnish for our peanut butter pie. Of course, with our focus on freshness and authenticity, we just had to go and make our own. Here's how we do it at Virgil's.

Peanut Brittle

Makes about 1 cup

¾ cup unsalted peanuts

2 tablespoons light corn syrup

¾ cup granulated sugar

⅛ teaspoon kosher salt

1 tablespoon unsalted butter

⅛ teaspoon baking soda

1. Preheat the oven to 350°F.

2. Spread the peanuts on a small cookie sheet and toast until lightly browned.

3. Combine all the ingredients except the peanuts and baking soda in a small saucepan with ¼ cup water. Bring to a boil and then whisk continuously until the mixture turns walnut brown. Remove it from the heat.

4. Immediately add the peanuts and baking soda. Stir until incorporated and then pour out onto a nonstick cookie sheet. (This has to be done extremely fast; the candy can overcook in a matter of seconds!) Let cool.

5. Once completely cooled, break the brittle into 1- to 2-inch pieces.

Key Lime Pie

This wonderfully simple taste delight teases the tongue with a tart citrus flavor and fresh smell that just screams, "Sunshine!" The strong citrus taste that dominates the pie is perfect for cutting through the heavier flavors of smoked or grilled meat. It's also a historic favorite, dating from the beginning of the twentieth century. Legend has it that by using regional key limes, a cook for a wealthy landowner was able to make and keep the pies without refrigeration. The original version makes good use of the tiny key limes found only in Florida, and the state made the origin of this special dessert official in 2006, when the Florida House of Representatives and Florida Senate decided to make the pie the Official Pie of Florida. About darn time, we say.

Serves 4–6

4 extra-large eggs, separated

2 tablespoons granulated sugar

2¾ cups condensed milk

¾ cup fresh-squeezed key lime juice (or substitute bottled key lime juice)

4 teaspoons key lime zest

1 teaspoon cream of tartar

1 premade graham cracker pie shell (or follow pie crust directions for the Perfect Peanut Butter Pie on page 287)

1. Preheat the oven to 225°F.

2. In a large mixing bowl, using a stand mixer or electric hand mixer, whip the egg whites and sugar until they form a firm meringue. Refrigerate.

3. In a clean mixing bowl, whip the egg yolks on high speed until they double in volume. Gradually add the condensed milk, lime juice, zest, and cream of tartar.

4. When all the ingredients have been thoroughly incorporated, gently fold in the chilled meringue. Pour the mixture into the pie shell.

5. Bake for 25 minutes. Remove to a wire rack to cool, and refrigerate overnight before serving.

Down-Home Chocolate Chess Pie

One of the grand things about the world of barbecue is that there is a story—sometimes a tall tale, sometimes true history, often a mixture of both—behind almost every recipe. Chess pie is no different, and most of the stories involve how the name came to be. Southerners prefer the version where a true Southern mother was asked before a cookout what she would be serving for dessert. The story goes that she said, "Jes' pie," meaning that she was serving just plain old custard pie. Of course the person on the other end heard it as "chess pie," and the name stuck. Call it what you will, chess pie is still a simple family favorite. You can add a lot of different flavorings to a chess pie, and in this recipe we've gone with tried-and-true rich chocolaty goodness. It dresses up the plain custard to make a rich and sumptuous treat for your tongue, and worthy of any story you want to tell about it.

Serves 4–6

4½ ounces bittersweet chocolate

2½ ounces semisweet chocolate

13 tablespoons unsalted butter

¼ cup heavy cream

2¼ cups granulated sugar

6 tablespoons all-purpose flour

½ teaspoon kosher salt

7 extra-large eggs

2 tablespoons plus 1 teaspoon pure vanilla extract

1 prebaked pie shell (or make your own Perfect Pie Dough shell, page 282)

¼ cup Simple Syrup (see Virgil's Bartending Tip on page 85), divided

1. Preheat the oven to 275°F.

2. Heat a double boiler over high heat until the water boils, and combine the chocolates, butter, and cream in the top. When the chocolate has completely melted, stir and set aside in a warm place.

3. Combine the sugar, flour, and salt in a medium mixing bowl, and thoroughly blend.

4. In a small bowl, lightly beat the eggs and vanilla. Incorporate into the flour mixture.

5. Fold the warm chocolate mixture into the flour mixture. Use an immersion blender or electric hand mixer to thoroughly blend all of the ingredients. The volume should increase by about one-quarter.

6. Pour into the prebaked pie shell. Place the pie in a rimmed sheet pan filled with about ¼ inch of warm water.

7. Bake for 25 minutes, then lightly spray the top of the pie with Simple Syrup that has been poured into a spray bottle. Bake the pie for an additional 45 minutes. Remove, spray with the rest of the Simple Syrup, and place on a wire rack to cool.

8. Refrigerate the pie overnight, and allow to warm to room temperature for 2 hours before serving.

Classic Lemon Chess Pie

A lot of Southern dishes can trace their roots to the British colonists who first ventured into the wild and beautiful lands of the South. Lemon Chess pie is one of those, a treat that evolved from the traditional English lemon curd pie. The original chess pie was plain custard, making it the perfect canvas for a host of other flavors and a chance for cooks everywhere to make it their own. Lemon, though, is the most natural flavoring for this dessert, and a great way to clean the palate after a big meal. The sweetness of the custard is cut perfectly with just the right amount of tart lemon, and the result is a little slice of heaven on a plate.

Serves 4–6

1 cup granulated sugar

2 tablespoons all-purpose flour

Pinch of kosher salt

1 tablespoon lemon zest

Juice of 1 lemon

1 teaspoon pure vanilla extract

2 egg whites

2 eggs

1 cup buttermilk

1 premade pie shell (or make a Perfect Pie Dough shell, page 282)

1. Preheat the oven to 350°F.

2. Combine the sugar, flour, and salt in the mixing bowl of a stand mixer, or in a large mixing bowl if using an electric hand mixer.

3. In a separate mixing bowl, combine the zest, lemon juice, vanilla, egg whites, eggs, and buttermilk. Add this mixture to the flour mixture, and blend with a paddle attachment until smooth.

4. Pour the filling into the pie shell. Bake for 35 to 40 minutes, or until firm. Remove to cool on a wire rack, and then refrigerate overnight before serving.

 # A Terrific Topping

As wonderful as the pies in this chapter are, we think that most are improved with the addition of a little homemade whipped cream. We like to spruce ours up a bit, but it's still the simplest, satisfyingest dessert topping you're likely to come across.

Virgil's Special Occasion Whipped Cream

1 tablespoon Simple Syrup (see Virgil's Bartending
   Tip on page 85)
1 cup heavy cream
½ teaspoon dark rum

Combine all the ingredients in a chilled nonreactive metal bowl and, using a chilled whisk, whisk until stiff peaks form. Serve immediately. Of course, if you're serving to children, omit the rum.

Virgil's Perfect Banana Pudding

If you're looking for a crowd-pleasing cookout favorite that will delight the kids in your family as well as everyone else, look no further. You should see the faces light up when we bring a big bowl full of this delicious sunshine-yellow concoction out to one of the Virgil's tables. This classic barbecue dessert is such a crowd favorite that there is even a National Banana Pudding Festival held every year in Tennessee! The secrets to all that popularity are abundant ripe bananas, a creamy texture, and genuine vanilla wafers. Buy bananas with a little speckling on them for a rich, deep sweetness that provides a satisfyingly natural flavor—something box mixes can't rival. (True Southern banana pudding is to mixes what gold is to brass.) We recommend you use real Nilla wafers, because bargain-brand vanilla wafers can reflect badly on the pudding.

Serves 4–6

2 small ripe bananas, peeled and chopped

¾ cup granulated sugar

1 ounce banana liquor (or substitute banana extract)

1½ teaspoons pure vanilla extract

2 tablespoons light corn syrup

1¾ cups heavy cream, divided

1 cup whole milk

½ cup all-purpose flour

2 egg yolks

Pinch of kosher salt

24–30 Nilla wafers, divided

2 large ripe bananas, peeled and cut on a slant into ½-inch-thick slices

2–3 sprigs mint for garnish (optional)

1. Bring the water in the bottom of a double boiler to a boil over medium-high heat.

2. In the top of the double boiler, combine all the ingredients except for 1½ cups of heavy cream, the wafers, and the large sliced bananas. Place over the bottom of the double boiler and whisk vigorously for about 10 minutes, or until the custard is thickened enough to stick to the whisk. Remove and refrigerate for at least 20 minutes.

3. Beat the remaining heavy cream until it forms stiff peaks. Do not overmix it.

4. Carefully fold the whipped cream into the cooled custard until combined and smooth. Be careful not to overmix.

5. Arrange a layer of the sliced bananas in the bottom of a casserole dish or serving bowl. Cover with a thin layer of pudding and top with a layer of wafers. Repeat the layers until you've used up the remaining ingredients. Crush several wafers and spread on top. Refrigerate for at least 4 hours prior to serving.

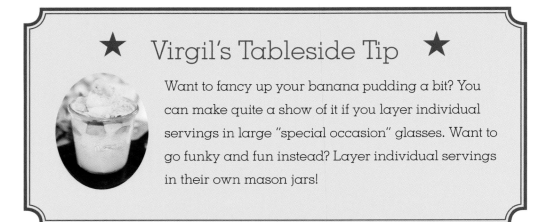

★ Virgil's Tableside Tip ★

Want to fancy up your banana pudding a bit? You can make quite a show of it if you layer individual servings in large "special occasion" glasses. Want to go funky and fun instead? Layer individual servings in their own mason jars!

Red Velvet Cake

If desserts could talk, this one would have some fascinating tales to tell. Legend has it that it owes its crimson color to World War II food rationing, when the most widely available food coloring was boiled beets—an addition that also helped keep the cake super-moist. Word of the recipe spread far and wide when a Texas-based extract company (who also happened to sell red food coloring) started promoting it across the country. Southern cooks put their own spin on the traditional butter-based French icing known as "ermine icing" to create easier but still delicious (and pretty) buttercream frostings. In any case, it's the type of icebox cake that brings to mind Mama's best baking. Rich, delicious, and the very best kind of sweet, this cake is also stunning enough to suit special occasions (it's even been used as a wedding cake). Chances are, your guests are going to be mighty impressed with the look . . . right before they polish it off!

Serves 4–6

Cake

1 teaspoon baking soda

1 tablespoon white vinegar

2 cups cake flour

1½ cups granulated sugar

1 tablespoon cocoa powder

½ teaspoon kosher salt

1 cup buttermilk

1 teaspoon pure vanilla extract

4 tablespoons red food coloring

½ cup unsalted butter, softened

2 extra-large eggs

Frosting

2 cups whole milk

½ cup all-purpose flour

2 teaspoons pure vanilla extract

½ teaspoon kosher salt

½ cup vegetable shortening

1 cup unsalted butter

3 cups confectioners' sugar, sifted

1. Preheat the oven to 350°F. Prepare a round 10 × 2-inch cake pan or springform mold by greasing it with butter and sprinkling with flour.

2. In a small bowl, dissolve the baking soda in vinegar. In a large mixing bowl, using a stand mixer or an electric hand mixer, combine the cake flour, sugar, cocoa, and salt.

3. In a separate bowl, combine the buttermilk, vanilla, and red food coloring.

4. Start the mixer on low and blend the flour mixture in the bowl. Add the buttermilk mixture, and then the vinegar mixture. When all the ingredients are fully incorporated, blend in the butter and eggs until the batter is smooth.

5. Pour the batter into the prepared pan and bake for 20 to 25 minutes, or until a toothpick comes out clean. Remove to a wire rack to cool.

6. To make the frosting, combine the milk, flour, vanilla, and salt in a small saucepan. Cook over low heat, whisking until thick. Remove and let cool.

7. In the mixing bowl of a stand mixer, or using an electric hand mixer, cream the shortening and butter. Add the confectioners' sugar and blend until smooth. Fold in the cooled milk mixture and blend until smooth.

8. When the cake has completely cooled, cut into three separate layers of equal thickness.

9. Spread a generous layer of the frosting on top of the bottom layer. Top with the second layer and another layer of frosting. Top with the third layer and spread the remaining frosting evenly over the top and sides.

Carrot Cake

A tip of our hats to the brave soul who first tried adding carrots to a dessert. We imagine people thought that particular baker was plum crazy, but it turns out that it was a stroke of genius. You see, carrots are some of the most naturally sweet vegetables, so it only makes sense to use them in a cake. They also add a lovely color and they even keep the cake nice and moist. When all is said and done, they're a pretty smart choice for a cake ingredient. We added a little burst of pineapple goodness and walnutty crunch to our version, and we dressed the moist, sweet cake with a super-simple cream cheese frosting. If you're feeling adventurous and creative, you can build on the cake and the frosting by adding flavors like almond or citrus or substituting pecans for walnuts in the cake. No matter what, the carroty goodness will remain. We promise.

Serves 4–6

Cake

2 cups granulated sugar

1½ cups canola oil

4 extra-large eggs

2 cups all-purpose flour

2 teaspoons ground cinnamon

1⅔ cups cocoa powder

2 teaspoons baking soda

½ pound carrots, peeled and shredded

½ pound diced fresh pineapple

1 cup chopped walnuts

2 teaspoons pure vanilla extract

Frosting

12 tablespoons unsalted butter

3 cups confectioners' sugar, sifted

1½ cups cream cheese

2 teaspoons pure vanilla extract

1½ cups toasted shredded coconut

1. Preheat the oven to 325°F. Prepare a round 10 × 2-inch cake pan or springform mold by greasing it with butter and sprinkling with flour.

2. Cream the sugar and oil in a large mixing bowl, using a stand mixture or an electric hand mixer set on medium. Add the eggs one at a time, and continue to mix until fully incorporated.

3. In a separate large mixing bowl, sift the flour and add the cinnamon, cocoa, and baking soda. Add the flour mixture to the eggs mixture. Blend until smooth.

4. Add the remaining cake ingredients and blend until incorporated.

5. Pour the batter into the prepared cake pan and bake for 1 hour, or until a toothpick inserted into the center comes out clean. Remove and cool on a wire rack, then remove from the pan.

6. For the frosting, cream the butter, confectioners' sugar, cream cheese, and vanilla in a large mixing bowl, using a stand mixer or an electric hand mixer. Blend on medium until smooth.

7. When the cake has thoroughly cooled, spread the frosting in a generous layer on top and then down the sides. Gently press the toasted coconut onto the sides and serve.

Pecan Pie

Legend has it that early French settlers invented pecan pie right after the natives in the region educated them on the flavor-rich nut. That may be so, but we Americans have certainly run with the ball since then. Today, pecan pies are not only a mainstay at Thanksgiving and Christmas feasts, they're also a longtime favorite around the barbecue table. All the popularity is due to the rich, almost smoky flavor of the pecans, and the decadent sweetness of the filling. We make our pecan pie the old-fashioned way—with the dense flavors of dark corn syrup and molasses, and just a couple simple spices. We think it's a good combination, because when we serve slices of this brown ambrosia, the forks are a-flying!

Serves 4–6

1 cup dark corn syrup

1 cup packed light brown sugar

1 tablespoon pure vanilla extract

3 tablespoons molasses

1¾ teaspoons ground cinnamon

¼ teaspoon kosher salt

5 extra-large eggs

1½ cups pecan pieces

1 unbaked deep-dish pie shell (or make your own Perfect Pie Dough shell, page 282)

3 tablespoons unsalted butter, chilled

1. Preheat the oven to 375°F.

2. In the bowl of a stand mixer, or a large mixing bowl if using an electric hand mixer, combine the corn syrup, sugar, vanilla, molasses, cinnamon, and salt. Beat on medium with a paddle attachment.

3. Add the eggs one at a time while continuing to blend. Mix until the ingredients are thoroughly incorporated.

4. Evenly distribute the pecan pieces on the bottom of the pie shell. Carefully pour the filling into the shell over the pecans.

5. Cut the butter into small pieces and distribute evenly around the top of the pie.

6. Bake for 10 minutes. Reduce the heat to 325°F, and bake for an additional 40 minutes. Remove and allow to cool on a wire rack before serving.

Deep Dish Sour Cream Apple Pie

Some people think of this purely delicious dish as the Southern version of streusel. Fact of the matter is, we think it's a whole lot better than that! The secret to this pie is the perfect partnership of apples and sour cream. Those two ingredients just seem to naturally go together like June Carter and Johnny Cash. Combine them in the pie and drop a spicy, sugary topping on the dessert and you have one irresistible mix of tart, sweet, creamy, crumbly, and crunchy. That's a lot of taste and texture for one dessert, and it's a heck of a way to end a cookout with a big bang.

Serves 4–6

Filling

2½ pounds (5 medium) Granny Smith
    apples, peeled, cored, and cut into
    ¼-inch slices

1 tablespoon ground cinnamon

1 teaspoon ground ginger

1 teaspoon ground allspice

5 tablespoons granulated sugar

4 tablespoons unsalted butter, melted

5 tablespoons all-purpose flour

½ cup plus 2 tablespoons heavy cream

¾ cup maple syrup

¾ cup sour cream

1 unbaked pie shell (or homemade
    Perfect Pie Dough shell, page 282)

Topping

1 cup light brown sugar

½ cup all-purpose flour

2 teaspoons ground cinnamon

1 teaspoon ground ginger

4 tablespoons unsalted butter

1⅓ cups pecan pieces

1. Preheat the oven to 325°F.

2. Thoroughly combine all of the filling ingredients in a large mixing bowl. Spoon the filling into the pie shell.

3. Mix the topping ingredients together in a large mixing bowl until combined into a coarse crumble. Spread on top of the pie.

4. Bake uncovered for 30 minutes. Reduce heat to 275°F and bake for an additional 30 to 40 minutes, or until the apples are tender and the top is golden brown.

Adult Favorites: Ice Cream Floats and a Milkshake

Who doesn't love a good ice cream float? And what barbecue fan would turn down a tasty beer? Combine the two, and you have some kind of scrumptious dessert that just seems perfectly suited to be the last stop on a menu of true barbecued dishes. This float is dominated by clean, light flavors of vanilla and orange, and it will please your sweet tooth and quench your thirst in one stroke. For those who don't particularly care for beer, we've included a couple adult beverage alternatives that use the same idea of a float, but with flavors that will appeal to different preferences.

Vanilla Porter Float

Serves 1

2 scoops high-quality vanilla ice
    cream
½ (12-ounce) bottle Breckenridge
    Vanilla Porter (or similar vanilla
    porter)
½ ounce Cointreau
1 Maraschino cherry, for garnish

Drop the ice cream in a large pint glass. Slowly pour in the beer, being careful that the foam doesn't run over the rim. Drizzle the Cointreau on top and serve, garnished with a cherry on top.

Apple Cider Float

Serves 1

2 scoops high-quality vanilla ice cream

½ (12-ounce) bottle Angry Orchard Hard Cider

½ ounce cinnamon schnapps

1 apple wedge, for garnish

Drop the ice cream in a large pint glass. Slowly pour in the cider. Drizzle the schnapps on top and serve, garnished with the apple wedge.

Chocolate Cherry Bourbon Milkshake

Serves 1

1 ounce bourbon

3 ounces whole milk

3 large scoops high-quality vanilla ice cream

1 tablespoon malt powder

¼ cup dark chocolate shavings

5 Maraschino cherries, chopped

Combine the first four ingredients in a blender, and thoroughly blend. Add the chocolate and cherries and blend for 2 to 3 seconds more. Serve in a pint glass.

11

Suggested Menus

Sometimes you're just not sure what you want to cook out. You might feel like having something smoked, but you don't have a real good idea of what side dishes will go best with your main course. Or maybe you just want to mix it up a bit—barbecue something you don't normally cook—and not have to sprain your brain thinking about the ideal menu. We get that, we really do. We put meals together for a living, so we understand how much work matching the right barbecue to the right side dishes and the perfect dessert can be. There's a bit of magic in the right combination of dishes and getting it just perfect can take a fair bit of thought and consideration. So we decided to make the process a little easier for you.

We've compiled some popular barbecue menus in this chapter, combinations of dishes that together make special meals that are greater than the sum of their parts. We've themed these for different occasions, but you can adapt them to any given day or celebration. The menus, like the recipes that make them up, are all about having a good time. One of the many great things about barbecue is how well it's suited to just about any event.

We hope you'll use these menus as a starting point. Replace a dessert here or a starter there as the mood moves you, to suit the crowd, or just accommodate your own taste bud preferences. Remember, the only wrong barbecue menu is the one that sends people home hungry.

The Traditional Barbecue Cookout

Few dishes say "barbecue" like a tried-and-true brisket, and few briskets are as tried and true as our True Texas Brisket. That's why it's the perfect centerpiece to an old-fashioned, rib-sticking, serious barbecue feast. We've included classics that just naturally go together, like the potato salad that's been served in Texas meat markets for about two days longer than forever, and our own take on the ultimate barbecue dessert, banana pudding. This meal is one strong flavor layered on another, with none of them competing for your tongue's attention, and these dishes are sure to leave all comers pleasantly full and happy.

Virgil's Smoked Chicken Wings with Blue Cheese Dip (page 47)
True Texas Brisket (page 173)
Pure and Simple Potato Salad (page 143)
Virgil's Perfect Banana Pudding (page 301)

Sunday Social Gathering

Sunday church socials and barbecue go hand-in-hand. Matter of fact, the smell of some good meat smoking over low heat brought many a worshipper to Sunday services back in the old South. These days, barbecue's still a great way to get people socializing, whether they're gathering out back of the church or in someone's backyard.

Don't matter where you are or how religious you might be, good barbecue is the centerpiece to wonderful social get-togethers. Amen.

Sunday Picnic Deviled Eggs (page 119)

Boston Butt, the Virgil's Way (page 217)

Grandma's Collard Greens (page 112)

Pure and Simple Potato Salad (page 143)

Perfect Peanut Butter Pie (page 287)

Special Birthday Celebration

Give the gift of delicious fulfillment to a loved one or friend on their special day. This well-rounded meal menu provides a little something for everyone at the birthday party, and there's something a little festive about all these dishes, from the firecracker spice explosion in the Creole Green Beans, to the signature fun crunch of the Kansas City Fried Chicken. Of course, a birthday wouldn't be a birthday without a cake to put the candles on, so we've included the fanciest dessert on our own menu—Red Velvet Cake. It's not only going to be a big taste hit, it even looks like a party favor!

Creole Green Beans (page 129)

Perfect Buttermilk Biscuits (page 141)

Kansas City Fried Chicken (page 235)

Perfectly Smoked Pork Loin (page 221

Red Velvet Cake (page 303)

A Game Day Spread

The secret to a great game day buffet is putting out dishes that don't require plates or utensils. The whole idea is food that can be eaten quick and easy while sitting in front of the TV or sharing some quality fan time at a big tailgate get-together. That's why we've put together a menu of finger foods that are finger-licking good. These are all fun eats, full of happy, crunchy, spicy, and smoky textures and flavors. You can throw in a vegetable platter if you like, just don't expect to see it polished off until these goodies are all gone. No matter who wins on the field, this menu is the ultimate score.

Virgil's Smoked Chicken Wings with Blue Cheese Dip (page 47)
Outrageous Barbecued Nachos (page 51)
Beer-Batter Onion Rings (page 145)
The Brisket Melt (page 190)

Sunny Saturday Grill Fest

Lazy Saturdays are custom made for a simple grilled feast. This particular menu is all about making a minimum of fuss with the cooking so that you can have a maximum of time to enjoy family, friends, or just lying in the hammock looking at the clouds. In keeping with the theme, the flavors in these dishes are simple and satisfying, just the basics that take care of any hunger and make the stomach pretty happy along the way.

Backcountry Cobb Salad (page 65)

Sunday Picnic Deviled Eggs (page 119)

Virgil's Hamburger (page 175)

Down Home Chocolate Chess Pie (page 293)

Good Ol' Fish Fry

Sometimes you just have a hankering for seafood that can't be denied. For hunger pains like those, we've put together a mix of taste delights from under the water. These include the incredibly rich bounty in our Maryland's Finest Crab Cakes, some gobble-them-up shrimp, and the hearty flavor of fried catfish. We threw in some classic sides that were pretty much invented to complement fish of one type or another. Finish your meal off with a palate-cleansing slice of Key Lime Pie and you may just find yourself dreaming of moving a little closer to the water.

Maryland's Finest Crab Cakes (page 37)

Popcorn Shrimp (page 43)

Crispy Hush Puppies (page 121)

Friday Night Fried Catfish with Tartar Sauce (page 255)

Virgil's Simple Slaw (page 121)

Key Lime Pie (page 293)

Super-Special Sunday Brunch

There's nothing better to cap off a nice, relaxing weekend than a lazy Sunday brunch. The key is to keep it light. On Sunday, we tend to take a break from beef (usually, because it was on the cookout menu the night before) and serve up simpler, fresher flavors and fare. A little bit of seafood, a little bit of chicken, a few vegetables, and a touch of citrus makes for a meal that can easily run right into late afternoon. And if you happen to miss church, well, we won't tell.

Ceviche de Camarones (page 149)

Oh-My-Gosh Jalapeños Rellenos (page 57)

Grilled Vegetable Salad (page 61)

Barbecued Halves and Quarters (page 249)

Mama's Peach and Blueberry Cobbler (page 285)

ACKNOWLEDGMENTS

This book was inspired by Artie Cutler's original road trips through the South, to discover the best barbecue in America. Artie was a visionary and remains an icon of the restaurant industry. The list of his restaurants reads like a guide to good eating in New York City: Murray's Sturgeon Shop, Dock's Oyster Bar & Seafood Grill, Haru, Ollie's Noodle Shops, Columbia and Time Square Bagels, Monsoon, Carmine's, and the subject of this book, Virgil's BBQ.

Artie passed away much too soon, leaving a lot of restaurant dreams behind. After Artie's death, his wife, Alice, took over as president of the company and keeper of Artie's vision. Since then, she has been not only an inspired leader, but a wise mentor and kind friend. Artie would be proud.

Alice has created a wonderful environment for this book to grow and develop, and CEO Jeffrey Bank has provided invaluable leadership to this process. He repeatedly reminded everyone involved with the book that it has to embody the Virgil's experience and the company's dedication to quality. Without his enlightened guidance, this would simply be an inferior book.

We acknowledge June and Steve Smith for starting Virgil's road trips by taking

Artie and Alice to Memphis and eating in seven BBQ restaurants/roadhouses in *one* day.

Many, many people played a part in getting the book to print, but special thanks are owed to some few key contributors to that effort.

Corporate Executive Chef Neal Corman is the true hero of this book, bringing his extensive expertise to the testing, retesting, refining and basically making every dish just as good as it could be. His desire and interest to create the best for the guests in our restaurants and the readers of this book translates into authentic recipes that bring the Virgil's cooking experience into your kitchen.

Corporate Director of Culinary Operations Glenn Rolnick is truly the eyes and the ears of all our restaurants. His synergy, dedication, and passion make him the best Executive Chef anyone could ask for. He, along with Alice and Jeff, are the heart and soul of the company. We should also thank Jeff's and Glenn's wives, the two Karens, for their encouragement. Their generosity and patience, especially through new restaurant openings, have allowed us to grow as we have.

The following people were also crucial to the book's success, and their importance should not be underestimated.

Beverage Director Erin Ward would prefer that you make yourself comfortable at one of our Virgil's bars, but has put the creativity and authenticity into the beverage recipes in this book that will make your home creations as special as the bar experience in our restaurants.

Thanks to Director of Operations, Michael Honea; Virgil's General Manager, Omar Zaras; Director of Human Resources, Espi Criscuolo; Director of Training, Genny Gomez; Director of Banquets, Penny Kaplan; Marketing Manager, Jennifer Wolinski; IT Manager, Max Lopez; and Virgil's Mohegan Sun Managing Partner, Cary Gilbert. It is thanks to the vision of one man that we are in the Bahamas, and have created the world's largest BBQ restaurant, and that man is Sol Kerzner. Thanks also to his team at Atlantis—George Markantonis, Ian Reid, and Paul O'Neil.

Thanks also go to Margaret Johnson, Virgil's Atlantis General Manager, and Amauris Pichardo.

Leading our accounting staff at Alicart is Drew Kuruc, along with Theresa Chang, Franz Steele, and their team. A special thanks to Jeffrey's assistant, who was often the glue that held the whole project together.

Agents Jane Dystel and Miriam Goderich knocked themselves out to get this book sold and see it come to life, and for that we will be eternally grateful. This book would not have become a reality without St. Martin's Press and the expertise of Elizabeth Beier, as well as her assistant Michelle Richter.

Thanks also to Alex Martinez, whose pictures truly capture the essence of Virgil's and barbecue. Thanks to Jeremy Deutsch and the rest of the guys at Deutsch, Metz and Deutsch. Additional thanks to Roy Tumpowsky, one of our trusted advisors, and to Dr. Jane Sullivan, of Sullivan and Associates, whose advice has always been insightful and valuable.

Last, but of course not least, thanks is given to Jody and Danielle Cutler, and Sarah and Andrew Bank, because family is truly everything.

INDEX